So You Wanna Be an
Be an
Artist?

So You Wanna Be an Artist?

WRITTEN BY A PROFESSIONAL ARTIST

Gianna Andrews

Published by Gianna Andrews Art
art@giannaandrews.com
giannaandrews.com

Gianna Andrews Art books are available at special discounts for
bulk purchase for sales promotions, premiums, fund-raising, and
educational needs. Special books or book excerpts also can be
created to fit specific needs. For details and permission requests,
write to the email address above.

ISBN 979-8-9872453-1-6 (hardback)
ISBN 979-8-9872453-0-9 (paperback)
ISBN 979-8-9872453-2-3 (eBook)

Printed in the United States of America

—

Developmental Editor: Fen Druadin
Copyeditor: James Gallagher
Cover Designer: Anna Dulaney
Cover Art & Illustrations: Gianna Andrews
Proofreader: Adeline Hull
Publisher & Book Designer: Kory Kirby
SET IN ADOBE CASLON PRO

Contents

Welcome

When you're lying on your deathbed, would you rather say "I am so glad I tried" or "I wish I had another chance"?

The choice is yours. Either you spend your time *living* what you want to be or *doing* what you don't want to do. I think it's fair to assume that if you're reading these words, you likely want to *be* an Artist. But perhaps you're stuck. You're wedged between a rock and a hard place . . .

The rock: you don't know how to become what you want to be.

The hard place: you're spending all your time doing what you don't want to be doing.

Are we on track here?

Well, you're in luck. I am here to help! After trudging off the beaten path of what I didn't want to be doing to become what I wanted to be, a Professional Artist, I've compiled all my experience into this book, just for you. Without receiving a college degree in art or attending business school, I not only became an Artist but built a successful business around my art.

Everything written here is from firsthand experience, compiled from many failures and successes. I've been a Professional Artist for over five years (painting for eight), and for the first time ever, I am laying out *how* I did what I did. I've created this blueprint so that you have something to follow on your quest to becoming an Artist.

Welcome to the "So You Wanna Be an Artist" club, my little *So You Wanna Be.* I am so happy you're here. To kick things off, let's define some important terms, defined by me for the purposes of this book.

Definitions

So You Wanna Be: someone who dreams about being an Artist or creates replicas of other Artists' work but is not yet an Artist.

Artist: someone who has a creative process and art practice integrated into their routine and an original style.

Working Artist: Artist who has a body of work, sells their art for profit, and also has a second job to support their livelihood.

Professional Artist: Artist who makes a full-time living off their art.

Creative process: the unique process of *how* an Artist creates their art.

Art: an Artist's final product, derived from their creative process.

Art practice: the creative space and time that an Artist routinely dedicates to their art.

Style: an Artist's defined and recognizable approach to their art and life.

Body of work: consists of more than a handful of art pieces that are cohesive and are developed through the creative process.

朱朱朱

I am not going to sugarcoat it—this ain't no cakewalk. But my hope is that, by reading this book and *applying* what you learn, you'll be well on your way from a So You Wanna Be to becoming a Professional Artist. You'll be unstuck from between that darn rock and a hard place. Buckle up, buttercup, because I am going to teach you how to *become* an Artist. If you stick with it long enough, the sky is the limit. And who knows? Becoming a Professional Artist might just be your future.

And without further ado, let's begin at the beginning—the Becoming.

CHAPTER 1

Becoming

I remember the moment I became a Working Artist. Years ago, I landed my first "real" commission project from the mom of one of my best friends. "Real" as in I was getting paid by a real client with real expectations that I needed to deliver upon. I think she saw the talent in me before I did. When she handed me an $800 check (the biggest check I'd made off my art), she said, "Don't expect it to be an easy road, baby. You're an Artist now."

Don't expect it to be an easy road, baby. Like the chorus from a hit song you can't forget, these words have replayed in my mind through the years. There couldn't have been more sincere words spoken to me at the moment when I became a Working Artist. It sealed the deal . . . solidified my path and pursuit of becoming a Professional Artist.

After all, I didn't sign up for this job because I thought it would be *easy*. I signed up for it because it felt like the only option. It's the road my soul chose, simple as that.

A few months after receiving this check, I quit my restaurant and catering jobs, moved out of my parents' house, and dove head-first off the Professional Artist waterfall with $8,000 to my name. I printed out my résumé with a list of service industry experience and kept it in my desk drawer for that first year of trying to make it as a Professional Artist. It was my backup plan in case my bills got too high and my pockets went dry. But I never ended up needing that résumé . . . my real career had just begun.

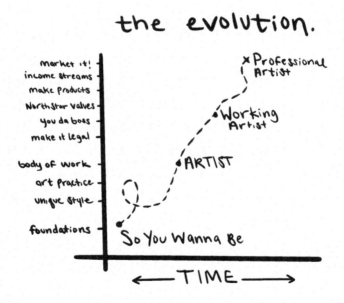

the evolution.

market it!
income streams
make products
Northstar values
you da boss
make it legal

body of work
art practice
unique style

foundations

x Professional Artist

• Working Artist

• ARTIST

So You Wanna Be

←— TIME —→

I believe that every human on this planet is capable of being an Artist. Part of being human is being creative. This doesn't just mean how you swirl a paintbrush or stroke a pencil. Creativity is how you structure your life, how you dress yourself, how you decorate your home, how you ski down a mountain, how you fix something that is broken. It's about the *process* of solving PROBLEMS and less about the final product.

Developing Your Foundations

First things first, before you can become an Artist, you must develop your own unique style. And *before* you can do that, you must build your **foundation of technique.**

How did you build your technique?

Growing up, I was a super creative kid. My favorite school projects were always those that involved my creativity, and I remember my mom and I spent a lot of time at home making crafts. But I never felt especially talented at art or painting. I wasn't a child art prodigy or anything. It wasn't until college that I followed my curiosity to build my art foundations.

Though I did not receive an art degree, I did take two college-level art classes as electives. The first was drawing, where I learned how to "draw what I see," or look at an object and attempt to re-create it on a large piece of paper. This class was helpful in learning how to draw at a larger scale, as before this I was only a hard-core doodler. I excelled quickly with the support of a professor who showed me how to work through roadblocks in my drawing.

The next semester I enrolled in a painting class. On the first day of class, we were instructed to do a warm-up activity: painting a glass mason jar. The oil paints were slippery and messy compared with the pencils and charcoal I had used in drawing. By the end of class my mason jar painting resembled more of a blob than a jar. I was hungry to learn, but I had zero technique. So I began asking questions. *How much solvent should I mix with the paint? When should I dip my brush? How much paint do I put on my palette?* It was here, painting more than eight hours per week, that my foundation of technique for painting was born.

Building a foundation of technique is the process of learning the tools for a given medium, which requires significant time and commitment. Over the years as an Artist, I haven't received instruction on much of anything, from my art to my business, but I credit these foundational art classes for my success as an Artist. They allowed me to drastically accelerate my technique. Since I was a child, I've always had this creative potential, but until that point I never had the proper instruction on technique to channel it.

If you are someone who would like to refine your technique, even if you aren't in a position to take a college-level art class, there are a lot of instructional options out there. You can find community art classes, online art workshops, and even YouTube how-tos. Ultimately, the source of your education doesn't matter, but I would highly recommend having a baseline of training because from here your style can truly start to shine.

Since you are reading this book about art, you very well *might* have a base-level foundation of technique already built in your favorite medium (you might like to paint with watercolors and know how to wet the paints, dip the brush, and stroke the brush on paper). This is a great place to start. Or perhaps you have a more developed technique. Wherever you are, now is a good time to assess your technique so that we can move forward into developing your style.

Developing Your Own Style

Hidden somewhere inside you is a unique style that ONLY YOU HAVE. A foundation of technique will increase your ability to express your style. However, no matter how much background training, how many certifications, or how much of a foundation of technique in the arts you have, your style can't be learned in a classroom. *It must be developed by you.* And if you wanna be an Artist, it is essential to spend time developing your own unique style.

I'll even go so far as to say that *your brain cannot choose, find, or decide your style*, because your style is sourced straight from your soul—a subconscious place. Through the years I've realized that my brain tends to get in the way of my own style. Our brains like to overthink and overcomplicate things. They think they can find all the answers from thinking, but it's actually the opposite. Your true style can't be found. You must allow it to come to you. Let me explain . . .

Remember that mason jar blob I painted on my first day of art class? That was at the very beginning of my painting journey, when I had only the bandwidth to focus on my technique, because my brain was learning how to use the tools of my medium. A month or so into the class, as I began to master my brush and palette, there was one day in particular where it all clicked into gear.

I stopped focusing on correctly handling the tools and almost began to zone out. It felt like meditation. Some call it flow state. My brain left the classroom. Everything felt fuzzy. I was no longer *thinking* about what I was painting. Instead, the art was flowing through me.

As I stepped back from that four-hour painting session to view my work, I almost couldn't believe what I had created. It was the first time I had ever *seen* an inkling of my own unique style before. And this was just the beginning of developing my style into what it is today. From that moment on, I became hooked on the feeling I had achieved from this creative flow state. The longer I could stay in it, the deeper I dove into developing my style.

Now don't get me wrong. I am not dropping into some deep-meditation flow state every single time I pick up my brush and palette. *Creativity is a fickle beast and tends to come and go as it pleases.* There are times that I get completely frustrated and roadblocked. There are times when I can't seem to access my style or flow state.

Sometimes this is because my thinking brain is getting in the way. But even through frustration, I continue to show up for my art.

In her book *Big Magic*, *New York Times* best-selling author Elizabeth Gilbert describes showing up to her desk like a farmer, diligently and consistently ready to work (in her case to write, but it applies to art as well).[1] Because if she waits for the inspiration to hit, she would seldom write at all. Some of what she writes may never be used in a published piece, but that's not the point. The point is that she shows up to her work day in and day out, rolls up her sleeves, and lives in service of her craft. She is there ready and willing to access that flow state when it decides to hit. **It's about the process, not the final product.**

After that painting class where I got the first inkling of my style, I spent two more years painting almost *every day*, for hours a day, developing my own style before I took my first job as a Working Artist. I was beyond passionate about painting. I was obsessed with mastering the art. I flowed with my creativity, and eventually my style strengthened and came out of the woodwork. Over the years my style has developed and evolved. I am an Artist, after all, I'm not supposed to stay stagnant. The point is that I constantly find I must surrender to the direction my soul chooses to lead my style, because I simply don't have a choice.

So you see, my lovely reader, the work doesn't begin at making your first paycheck from your art. It begins right here. First you

---

1 Before becoming a Working Artist, I would highly recommend reading *Big Magic*. It was groundbreaking for me at the beginning of my career.

must allow your style to come to you. Only then can you become an Artist. Double down on what makes your art unique to you, what makes YOU unique to you, and leave the rest behind. Your style, at its core, will fuel everything else from this point and beyond as an Artist. Don't let the pressure of the outside world squelch the true time and work it takes to develop your own style. "Art" created by the ego, or thinking brain, burns out quickly, like a sheet of paper in a flame, whereas creativity sourced from the soul burns slowly, like a local beeswax candle. You *must* be deeply passionate about your creative process to allow your style to come to you.

Your Creative Process

The more time you spend creating, the more you will begin to trust your unique process for creating your art. It's all about building trust with your process and yourself.

In the beginning, as a So You Wanna Be, you won't have your creative process dialed in. You are in the experimental phase. My best advice? Have fun with it! Try colors! Use black and white! Throw paint at the wall. Find what works for you. The more you can enjoy the creative process, the stronger your style will become.

As an Artist, you will develop your own creative process. However, even as an Artist, there is nothing wrong with revisiting your creative process and spicing things up. Maybe you've always played music while creating, but now it's time to throw on a podcast instead. Little shifts such as this can help us drop into our creative process.

There are two main phases to my creative process: conceptualization and execution.

Conceptualization

Conceptualization is the planning phase in which you create the plan for the art piece. This is always the hardest part of the process for me! It's time to get quiet and sift through my mind to see which painting wants to be created next. I usually look through my camera roll to see if I have snapped any good pictures from recent adventures. I use Google Images and royalty-free photos to enhance the developing concept.[2] Occasionally I have a vision for a painting pop into my head, colors and all, and this speeds up my conceptualization process. Sometimes coming up with a finalized concept can take me hours, as my brain likes to overthink this part of the process.

Some Artists create directly from their imaginations, while others prefer to create realistically from photos. I would categorize myself as falling somewhere in the middle. I like to use reference photographs when I am in the beginning phases of a piece, especially when I am laying out the concept. After the initial layers are laid on a painting, I put the images aside and let my creativity and style take over.

---

2 It's great if you can take your own photos and use your own experiences as reference for creating your art. If you want to paint directly from a photo, there are royalty-free photos you can find online to avoid copying (more on this in the "Copying Other Artists" section).

Since I have been painting for many years now, I have developed layouts and concepts that I play with and build on from piece to piece. My paintings usually evolve off one another.

Execution

This is the fun part! Once you've got your art concept dialed in, it's time to execute it. Set the vibes with music, candles, maybe some twinkly lights, whatever helps you feel inspired! This is when I drop into my flow state. I use acrylic paints, and they require many layers to get to the deep and vibrant colors I like. Most of my paintings take from ten to fifty hours from start to finish (depending on how large they are and the amount of detail). Needless to say, I spend a lot of time in the execution phase, but I love it! I typically listen to music or podcasts to keep my thinking brain entertained so that my subconscious creativity can flow, and I drop into that flow state even deeper.

Everyone's creative process is likely to be different, but I'll share an outline of mine:

1. Get quiet with myself and see if any ideas are top of mind.
2. Search for concepts in my phone camera roll, Google Images, and royalty-free images online.
3. Settle on reference photographs to inform piece.
4. Sketch concept on iPad (paper works too) based on reference photos *and* imagination.
5. Select canvas.

6. Select paint colors and brushes.

7. Set the vibe with music, a candle, and an open window.

8. Paint away!

9. Break down and experience self-doubt, hating the painting and feeling upset.

10. Keep painting.

11. Drink water—hydration is important!

12. Paint more.

13. Ask, "Am I done yet?"

14. Take a few days off.

15. Get back to it: "A few more lines here and here. Some more highlights here."

16. Finish: "Annddd I'm done!"

17. Hang masterpiece on wall.

When Self-Doubt Seeps In

Let's talk about an important point that can't be brushed by: number nine on our creative process outline. Even as an Artist, I can't count the number of times I have started a painting and a few hours in felt as though it was the ugliest painting *ever*—and why the heck did I choose this concept and these colors?

This, my friends, is called self-doubt. And self-doubt most definitely comes from your thinking brain, not your beautiful, wild soul. When self-doubt seeps into your creative process, it's your job to recognize it and then *keep creating.* **Don't let it stop**

you. Don't give your power away to the silly, pointless self-doubt. It's just here to keep you small . . . but you didn't show up to your creative process to stay small. You showed up to create gloriously mind-shattering art.

And guess what? Every Artist—heck, every human—has experienced self-doubt. No matter how successful one might be, it's an utterly human trait. I find that it's a constant practice of surrendering to my creative process and trusting myself and my art. It's not easy to move through self-doubt . . . but you can do it!!!

Seeking Inspiration from Other Artists

During my college-level painting classes, after being assigned our first big painting project, we were instructed to look back on the works of renowned Artists through history and select several of their pieces to aid in our conceptualization process. We were then to combine several pieces to use as reference suggestions for our own projects, while forming our own original concepts based on these reference images. These were the days before the iPad and Apple Pencil, and I remember printing out several paintings, cutting out different elements from them, gluing them into my notebook, and then drawing on top of them to form an original concept for my next painting.

When you seek inspiration from other Artists' work, you are still forming your own original concept. Copying another Artist's work is when you directly reference an Artist's work and do not form an original concept (we will cover copying in the "Copying Other Artists" section). The difference between seeking inspiration from other Artists and copying other Artists is a fine line. In my opinion, seeking inspiration is okay under the right circumstances, but copying is *never* okay.

Seeking inspiration from other Artists' work while you are a So You Wanna Be is helpful in developing your own foundation of technique and style. It can be helpful in the conceptualization and execution phase of the creative process, to inform you how to create your own unique style. However, if you have been a So You Wanna Be for quite some time and are ready to make the jump to being an Artist, I would highly recommend you move away from using other Artists' work as reference photos for your own work. To become an Artist, you must develop your own style, and after a while, using other Artists' work as a reference will inhibit the development of your own style. As we discussed above, painting directly from an array of photographs, whether those be from your camera roll or royalty-free images on the internet, can be a great way to integrate references into your creative process if you like to create from pictures.

If you find yourself unable to shake other Artists' work from your psyche, perhaps you would benefit from deleting Pinterest, Instagram, and TikTok apps from your phone so that you can take a break from looking at other Artists' work and hone in on a style that is authentic to YOU. I have also heard Artists say that they often compare themselves to other creators on the internet and feel impostor syndrome, as though they could never be as "good" as that Artist.

Sigh

As my partner, Kory, will often say, "Comparison is the death of joy." Well, I'll elaborate on that. *Comparison is also the death of creativity.* If you feel impostor syndrome, this is another sign that you might need to take some space from internet apps. Remember, you have a uniqueness to you that NO ONE ELSE IN THE WORLD HAS. You just need to allow space and time for the inspiration from your soul and the world surrounding you to speak to you. From this place, move forth and create art.

By the time you become an Artist, you will have your own creative process established and your own unique style defined. And as an Artist, you will no longer *need* to look at other Artists' work for you to create your own work, since you yourself are established in your own style. However, it is only natural for humans to inspire other humans, for art to inspire art, and for creation to evolve. Giving a shout-out to an element derived from another Artist's work in your own work is acceptable as long as your overall concept is *original*.

Musicians do this all the time; they add in a lyric from another musician's song as a shout-out to that musician, but the song is still their own original concept. I began adding in the style element of retro stripes into my paintings a few years back. Obviously I did not invent these stripes. But when I use them in my art and integrate them into my original concepts and unique style, I am throwing a reference to the seventies while maintaining my originality.

Whose responsibility is it to ensure your concepts are original?
As an Artist, it's your responsibility to be honest with yourself. Are you creating your own original concepts? Art is so subjective. It's up to our individual integrity to decipher the difference between seeking inspiration from other Artists and copying them.

Copying Other Artists

I want to help you become the best version of an Artist you can be. I want your original, creative, unique, unyielding style to shine bright and true to the colors of **you**. So that you may "wow" audiences for generations. How do you do this? *By creating original concepts.*

Obviously, you can't copy your way to getting there. And I know you, my dear reader, would never copy. But just so we are on the same page of what it means to copy another Artist, let's take a closer look.

What does it mean to copy another Artist?
Copying means to directly reference another Artist's work when creating a piece, and then take credit for that work. The art is owned by the original Artist, and the copycat is stealing said art.

Example 1: The copycat types in "mermaid" on Pinterest and finds an epic mermaid drawing. Next they draw it line for line on their page.

Example 2: The copycat sees a really cool painting on Instagram by one of their favorite Artists. They pull out their paints and a canvas and re-create the piece. They might change a few colors and move around the subject matter, but the copied piece is clearly directly referenced from the original piece.

If you wanna be an Artist, you know by now your style and original concepts are essential pieces of the pie. And, unfortunately, those who do copy are only doing a disservice to themselves.

🌲🌲🌲

My art has been copied many times throughout my career. I have seen my paintings and my Artist friends' paintings directly copied and posted on Instagram, with no reference to the original creator. I have even seen these pieces posted for sale. And I am not gonna lie—it feels like a tiny piece of me has been stolen when this happens. But I stay grounded in my belief that the universe is abundant and there is plenty to go around. So I keep my head high, keep painting, and move on. I prefer to live by example. I try not to let it be more than a blip on the screen.

🌲🌲🌲

Art belongs to the intellectual property of the original creator. Legally speaking, based on copyright law, directly copying or closely referencing another person's art and then selling/marketing said art is **illegal**. Morally speaking, taking credit for copied work is wrong. It is stealing art from the Artist.

I know this sounds harsh, and, hey, we are all human, and we all make mistakes. *This is just an important reminder to remain aware* and fix your mistakes once you realize you've made them.

I'll be honest. I made a copying mistake in the past. Back when I was still a So You Wanna Be, before I became an Artist, I used a reference photo for a painting of dripping lips I found on Pinterest, created by a digital artist. The painting I made came out so well that, at the time, I was very proud of it. It also looked very similar to the reference photo.

Soon after completing this painting, I got my first opportunity to hang my artwork at a local photography gallery for an upcoming ski swap event. I was so excited. I brought in eight pieces of my best work, all of which I was really proud. Seven of the eight were authentic to me and my style—they were original concepts that I had created. One of the eight—the lips—was not. Even though I was proud of that painting, it wasn't my concept, and *deep down I knew that.* But I was just a no-name painter, so who would really notice or care that the concept wasn't mine?

There I was, taking credit for art that wasn't my own on the wall of a photography gallery. The worst part of the show was that out of all my pieces, everyone LOVED the lips the most. Friends who owned a small ski company even wanted to put them on a pair of skis. So after the show, I sent them the high-res file, and they made a ski prototype.

Once I saw the skis in real life, I had a "coming to Jesus" moment. I thought to myself, "Oh my god, what if I get famous for this design, and it blows up, and then the original creator of the artwork sues me for stealing their design?" or "What if everyone finds out that I am a phony?"

Right then and there I called the guys at the ski company, told them the whole story, and asked them to discontinue the print. After that they didn't print any more skis with that art on them, and I removed that painting from my portfolio. I ended up giving the original painting to a past roommate and moved on from the whole ordeal.

In short, I learned that it's always better to create art that comes *authentically* from my style and creativity, because you never know which piece you put out into the world might gain attention. It's always better if it comes from your heart, not someone else's. Once you mess up, there's always a chance to fix your mistake.

Teachers and Mentorship

Receiving guidance from a teacher or mentor who is further along in the direction you want to go will accelerate your growth in that area and can quickly uplevel your skill. For example, here you are wanting to become an Artist and reading this book about *how* to become an Artist . . . you've already begun the process of receiving guidance in the direction you want to go. I was extremely fortunate to have a few teachers and mentors who helped shape my path from a So You Wanna Be to an Artist.

Above I discussed how my foundation of technique was established during the college-level painting-and-drawing classes. I was that overly curious kid in the art class who couldn't stop asking questions. I remember the professor saying to me, "There are other students in this class. I cannot just keep answering all of your questions."

Halfway through the semester, our professor swapped out with a different professor, who had a lot more patience for my inquisitive nature. With more of my questions answered, my skill accelerated quickly and culminated in my capstone piece. I had learned to paint the visions inside my head, since I now had a foundation of technique that is essential before developing a style.

Halfway through an environmental degree in college, I considered changing my major to art, but I didn't want to start over on a degree and acquire student loan debt. What was I to do with my life? I wasn't sure if being an Artist was feasible, so I enrolled in a National Outdoor Leadership School mountaineering course and flew halfway around the world to the Himalayas. Maybe I wanted to be a mountain guide? But even after forty-five days of trudging through this remote mountain range, I found myself dreaming of painting in the safety of that art classroom. I *missed* creating. So after three months of mountaineering and extended travel, I flew back to Montana, picked up my paint set, and began painting while attempting to reorient amid culture shock.

That was when Rachel Pohl entered my life in nothing short of divine timing. The first time we hung out, we went downhill mountain biking. On our second run, I went sailing over the handlebars, scorpioned my spine, and broke my back. My front teeth were shattered, and my entire body was abraded. After an hour-long ambulance ride to the hospital, I lay there in the ER, strapped to a stretcher with Rachel standing above me. At the time, her professional art career was just beginning to blossom.

I asked her with tears in my eyes, "What am I going to do now?"

She responded, smiling, "You're just going to paint."

And that's just what I did. At that moment, right then and there, there was no turning back.

I spent ten brutally painful but also strangely inspiring days in the hospital, surrounded by Rachel, my parents, and friends. I didn't stand up for the first five days. The following five days were spent learning to walk with a rigid clamshell back brace. It was the most literal and metaphorical rebirth of my entire life. I am not sure whether I had an inflated sense of confidence from the delirium of painkillers, but life was giving me a second lease, and I decided I was going to BE an Artist. I think I probably declared the news to everyone who set foot in my hospital room.

Further inspiring me, Rachel purchased one of my recent paintings, *Nanda Devi*, inspired by my mountaineering trip. I had no idea what to charge for something like that, but she wrote me a check for $450.

I was astounded. "That's way too much!"

She just laughed. "You have talent. This is how much it's worth."

I couldn't believe it. It felt like a fluke. *Would I ever sell a painting for that much ever again?* The answer, I later learned once my career began, was yes, eventually, many times over. Thanks to Rachel's encouragement and mentorship, for the first time ever, I believed it was possible to become an Artist, maybe even a professional one day.

I used my recovery to practice my craft, painting every day. I dropped half of my college course load so that I could have more time for physical therapy and painting. Rachel and I spent multiple days a week painting together. Having a painting buddy helped me remain accountable to a consistent creative practice, which accelerated the process of honing in on my unique style.

After my accident, Rachel and I were bonded. I had gone through the hardest time in my life, and she hadn't left my side. I learned about being a Working Artist by observing her methods. She taught me how to get my art photographed and made into prints and how to package my prints. She shared with me how she priced her products. I watched how gracefully she carried herself in her art career and in the world. Everywhere we went in public, someone stopped her to tell her how amazing her art was.

I had never been around someone who drew so much positive energy into their life from their own creativity. I was beyond inspired. Rachel helped me believe in myself and my craft. She showed me that being an Artist was a legitimate path, and I wouldn't be the Professional Artist I am today without her encouragement. I am so grateful for how this mentorship has blossomed into a friendship that Rachel and I share to this day.[3]

---

3 rachelpohlart.com / @rachel.pohl

Years later, after this huge external expansion of becoming an Artist, I had some internal growing to do. Once I had met my goal of becoming a Professional Artist, I had "made it," but in some ways the real work had just begun.

My art career has been a process of trusting the universe, but no matter how "enlightened" this might sound, the waters of the universe feel murky at times, and I needed guidance. So, when the pandemic hit in 2020, I took a course by Lindsay Mack with Tarot for the Wild Soul.

Her teachings opened my eyes to the difference between my brain and my soul, and to the duality we live as humans having both. Her teachings gave me the courage to trust myself and my inner knowing, both creatively and in business. One of the most influential parts of her teachings was that *we are all our own teachers* in this life. With this lesson, I was able to focus on defining myself in who I am as both a human and an Artist. I began following the direction I felt called, no matter what someone else might think about it.

After all, I bet some of the things I say in the book won't ring true for you. That's totally okay. As Lindsay would say, *Take what resonates and leave the rest.*

Art Degrees and College Debt

Do I need a college degree to become an artist?
Absolutely not. However, I am a proponent for classes or teachers that help you build your technique. But you do not need to go to a

fancy art school to do this. While art schools may be a great place to develop your foundation of technique and even your style, they often do not teach about the business of selling your art (we will cover this later in "The Business"). To be a successful Professional Artist in this day and age, not only do you need art skills, but you also need business skills. However, if you choose not to pursue higher education in art, you *must* put in the time and care it takes to develop your technique and style. You cannot skip this step and expect to become an Artist.

I am glad I decided not to go to art school, as in my situation it would have required taking out student loans. I was privileged to have a budget provided by my parents to go to a state college, but if I had tacked on the additional years of art school, not only would I have acquired debt, but I was worried I might fall behind on my journey to become an Artist. I wanted to enter the real world and become an Artist then and there.

Debt can be a dream crusher when you are starting out as a Professional Artist, as these monthly payments add to your cost of living, making it more difficult to rely on a volatile income. I am not saying it's impossible to become a Professional Artist with student loans. I am just saying that it's more challenging. And as we will discuss later, when you decide to become a Professional Artist, it is best to lower your costs as much as possible.

I know several successful Professional Artists who received a college degree in art. But I also know people who received an art degree and are not Professional Artists, nor do they practice art much at all anymore. Receiving a college degree in art does not ensure that you will be able to "make it" as a Professional Artist. If you want to be an art teacher or professor, a university setting is definitely the place to go. If you want to sell your art, it might not be. It's a mixed bag, and it's up to you to decide what's best for you.

In my five-plus years of being a Professional Artist, no one has ever asked to see my degree, and no one seems to care that my degree isn't in art. I do believe receiving a college degree in environmental studies taught me a level of professionalism I lacked beforehand; plus I am also passionate about the environment, which does seep into my artwork. However, does my degree directly apply to my career? No. The art business world is a bit more cut-and-dried than the minutia of a college education. It's all about relationships, who you know, and whether you know how to do your taxes!

CHAPTER 2

The Practice

So you dream of being an Artist, but do you have your art practice and routine established? You can't be an Artist if you don't have an art practice . . . it's fundamental to the definition of the craft.

Creative Time and Space

Over the years as a Professional Artist, I've heard people say, "Oh, I sure miss creating art. I used to do it all the time, but now I don't have the space." Or, "Back in college I made a lot of art, but now I can't find the time." Or, "Now that I moved into my new place, I don't have room for art. I miss it."

So here's a little wake-up call for you, my lovely So You Wanna Bes . . . there likely will never be the *right* space, and there will most definitely never be *extra* time. I am a huge believer that you create your own reality. By voicing to the universe that you don't have the right space or enough time, you most definitely *never* will. But here's the good news—you can change this story in your head and thus transform your reality. It's time to debunk this limiting belief!

Just like beginning a workout program for the first time in years, you can't head out of the gate expecting to run a marathon. First, you need to run a mile, then two miles, five miles, . . . if you're going to build or rebuild confidence in your creative discipline, it's important to set little milestones.

Let's start with your **creative space**. I can't even begin to explain how important this is if you wanna be an Artist.

But I don't have room to set up a creative space . . .

Is that *really* true? Sure, maybe you can't paint a huge two-by-four-foot painting in your small bedroom, but can you start on paper, or with a small canvas? Find a corner of your bedroom, apartment, living room, kitchen, or garage—whatever you have—and set up a table there (a small table works just fine). Dedicate this table to your art and *your art alone*. Once you've set it up, it's best if you can leave the table in place as a dedicated home for your creative process. Set up your supplies and organize your brushes and pencils in jars. Put your paints in a container. Get a comfy chair. Set up a little speaker or put your headphones on if the space is noisy. Make the space feel like *you*. Now the fun begins—it's time to create!

Why do I need a dedicated art table?

Well, if you set up all your art supplies on the kitchen table and then it's time for dinner, you'll have to spend extra effort to move the supplies off the table, not only taking up your precious time but also limiting the chances you might set up your art supplies there to create again. By having a dedicated art table, your brain is much less likely to make excuses about *why* you can't make your art—because your art table is literally always there, patiently waiting for your crafty hands.

Once I decided to dedicate myself to my art, my creative table became integral to the frequency of my painting practice. It was my junior year of college, and I was living in a house with two other roommates. I turned the desk in my bedroom that I used to study for school into my art table. I set up an easel next to it. My desk chair also served as the chair I sat in to paint at the easel. Sure, it was crammed in my bedroom. My easel covered up the small TV I had in the corner, and my paints got all over my desk and onto my computer whenever I tried to do homework. But the important part was that my paints and brushes had a home! I'd go to class, to the climbing gym, or to work at a sandwich shop for $8.50 an hour plus tips and return home to my creative space. There was no excuse I could make about not painting, so I'd settle in and paint.

Not long after breaking my back, I got super into rock climbing.

My physical therapist said it would strengthen my back muscles around the smooshed vertebrae, so once I was cleared to do so, I went to the climbing gym almost every day. Not ten months after breaking my back, I was on a climbing trip in Red Rocks, rolled my ankle, and broke my foot. My climbing partner had to carry me out two miles.

The break was just a hairline fracture, nowhere near as traumatic as my broken back, but it was a serious wake-up call. Was I going to be an Artist? Or was I going to keep breaking myself in my attempt to be an outdoor athlete? Did I even *want* to be an athlete at the level I was trying to be an athlete? The answer was no.

In the midst of this existential crisis, I decided to move back to Washington and in with my parents. I needed a reset. I was tired of being a patient in the waiting room. And, honestly, I needed my mom. So I convinced the university to allow me to take my classes remotely and graduate from afar (something no one was doing prepandemic).

Back at my parents' house, my creative space inevitably moved with me. I set up my painting zone in the corner of their living room (they didn't want me to paint in my bedroom for fear of getting paint on the carpets). It was there, with the support of my family and the familiarity of the Pacific Northwest, that I began to become an Artist. My creative space was an integral piece to my success in developing my style, and once I dedicated more time, my body of work (discussed in the next section) really began to develop.

⼨⼨⼨

Okay, enough rambling, back to you! Now that you've got your space set up, it's time to assess your creative time. Your creative table should give you a bit of extra time for your art, since setting up your supplies used to take about ten minutes, and breakdown took ten minutes. Now you have twenty extra minutes to add to your creative time. Boom. You're welcome.

But life is busy . . . I don't have any extra time!?

Don't get me wrong—I know life is busy. Especially if you have children and other responsibilities that require your care and attention, it can be difficult to carve out time to create. But as we established before, there will never be more time, and you will never have enough of it, so you must **make the time**.

Let's take a closer look at where you spend your time. How much time do you spend scrolling social media daily? Thirty minutes? Three hours? When do you usually scroll? In the morning? Or at night before bed? How much time do you spend socializing per week? What would it look like if you converted this time into creating? Maybe that would mean creating for twenty minutes in the morning while you drink your coffee before the workday. Maybe that would mean creating for an hour after work before you make dinner.

It doesn't matter when you do the creating. But what does

matter is the habit you make around your creative process and the boundaries you set with yourself, the internet, and others to preserve your creative time. Consistency is key.

Body of Work

Now that you've established your creative space and have set aside creative time, if you'd like to transition from an Artist to a Working Artist, and maybe even to a Professional Artist, it's time to create a body of work.

A body of work consists of more than a handful of original pieces or more that are developed during your creative process in your own style.

Each original you create within your body of work should be different. Let your style evolve from one piece to the next. Do NOT repeat the same design but DO take elements from one piece to the next, as this will help solidify your style. The minute you begin watering down your designs is the minute you begin undervaluing your own creative genius as an Artist. *Think outside the box.* Spend time and care in the conceptualization phase (as we discussed before).

Why do you need a body of work?

1. Art is strongest and most impactful when there are multiple pieces to back it up.
2. It will differentiate you from other Artists, legitimizing your own style and work.

3. It will act as your portfolio as you continue to grow as an Artist.
4. It will serve as a basis for who you are as an Artist.
5. Once you become a Working Artist, you will be busy with business logistics, especially in the beginning. It's best if you have a portfolio of work to lean on to use on products for marketing and branding (more on this in Chapter 3).
6. This work could be displayed at galleries and other venues.

The first body of work I created consisted of eighteen pieces and took me two to three years to create. Some of these pieces I had created early on while I was still developing my style. For this body of work, I selected my *best work*. I left out the pieces that I didn't feel I had executed properly to fit my style. In fact, it was once these eighteen pieces were hung next to each other at my first art show at evo, Seattle, that I was able to see my own unique style.

Dedication

When I decided to dedicate myself to a life of art at the fresh age of twenty-one, my friends were going out to bars and partying on the weekends, and I was in my bedroom at my art table desk, painting. After class, you would find me painting. After working late nights in the sandwich shop until 10:00 p.m., I was painting. When I realized I wasn't painting enough, I moved back in with my parents so I could focus deeper on painting. **I changed the**

entire structure of my life to accommodate my art practice. I had the vision, I made the decision to stick to it, and I put it into action. And guess what . . . it worked. My dedication paid off. You know why? Because I was *passionate* about it. I was deeply driven to become an Artist.

It's probably not worth changing around your whole life unless you *love* art. But if you are passionate about your craft, when there is a will, there is *always* a way. And if you purely wait for inspiration to hit, the truth is, you're likely never to build a body of work or become an Artist. You must set aside space and time to dedicate yourself to your creativity.

How do I know when I've become an Artist?

You've been dedicated enough to develop your foundation of technique and your style, hone in on your creative process, establish an art practice with creative space and time, and create a body of work. Now you've met all the requirements to "become" an Artist, right?

Well, mostly, but there's one more *essential* step in the process: you must believe that you are, in fact, an **ARTIST.** Because here's the thing . . . there won't be a grandiose moment when the world bows down at your feet and bestows the title of Artist upon you. **No one else can make you an Artist.** No one else can decide when you've transitioned from a fresh, little So You Wanna Be to a true Artist.

Even if someone calls you an Artist, it doesn't mean you are an Artist. And if someone says you aren't an Artist, that isn't necessarily true either. Honestly, it doesn't matter what anyone else thinks about the matter. Only you can define your truth. So are you an Artist yet? Only you know the answer. If you are, wear it proud, my friend.

It took me a long time to build up the confidence to call myself an Artist. There was a lot of learning I had to do between deciding I was going to become an Artist while lying in that hospital bed to actually *becoming* one. I don't think I began to entertain calling myself this title until I began selling my work. But once I declared my title as an Artist, there was no going back. I believed that I was an Artist, so the rest of the world began to believe it too.

Creating Your Daily Schedule

Once I made the leap to being a Professional Artist, all decisions that needed to be made became *mine to make*. From the littlest decisions of when to start my day, to when to take a lunch break, to huge decisions like whether I wanted to work with a certain brand, or if I should invest thousands of dollars on a product . . . *everything was on me*. I remember this time clearly; it was like being in full control of my life but also in zero control at the same time. I was at the mercy of funding my livelihood off my art.

At first I attempted to run my art business out of a van. I wanted zero structure and just wanted to paint and live a hippie-artist-surfer lifestyle with my boyfriend. So romantic, right?

Like a hot and heavy summer fling that burns out quickly, this dream lasted about a month (the boyfriend is still sticking around, though).

Here I am, years later, and I still live a minimally structured life. Because I know that for me, I need the slightly unstructured hours and days to allow my creativity to flow. But the truth is, living out of a van with no creative space and no idea where I was going to find Wi-Fi—let alone sleep, use the bathroom, or eat next—was hard on me. I quickly realized it was taking energy away from my business. So my boyfriend and I moved out of the van and got a rental. And that was also one of the best decisions I could have made for my career as a Professional Artist. The lesson was that, for me, I need a home base for my business and creativity to function.

You see, being self-employed takes a lot of *self-awareness*. It requires us to be assertive and honest with ourselves. We must be okay with learning from our failures. We have to be able to say, "Wow, this idea I had isn't working. I am going to go back to the drawing board and try something different."

So even if you're like me and you don't love "routine," I'm here to tell you, whether you would like to become a Working Artist or a Professional Artist, you need to create some type of routine. When you're running a business, every day is likely to be a little different, because you really have three jobs instead of one. It's important to have your routine work for you to help you get the job done.

Pro Tip: Spend fifteen minutes every evening detailing your schedule for the following day in a "daily notebook" (this is just a spiral-bound notebook with lined pages). Write down everything you plan to do the next day. And I mean everything: when you plan to shower, when you will exercise, when you will respond to emails, when you will market, and when you will create your art. If you are also working another job, you can include those hours in this list as well. The more detailed the better. Then, the next day, cross items off the list as you go. Once I started doing this, I made leaps and bounds in my productivity. I've probably gone through at least twelve daily notebooks by now.

Example Daily Schedule List:
- 7:00 a.m.: Wake up.
- 7:15 a.m.: Drink water/coffee.
- 7:45 a.m.: Take morning walk.
- 8:30 a.m.: Answer emails/admin.
- 10:00 a.m.: Attend meeting.
- 10:30 a.m.: Do admin.
- Noon: Take lunch break.
- 1:00 p.m.: Paint.

- 5:00 p.m.: Work out.
- 6:00 p.m.: Eat dinner.
- 7:30 p.m.: Paint.

Since this is your little universe (more on this in Chapter 3), some days this schedule might include less work, and some days it might include more. It's important to build in activities to your daily life that fill you up so you don't burn yourself out working nonstop.

Some days an item may come up that requires your immediate attention, throwing off your schedule. That's totally okay, and honestly that's life. The point of the daily schedule is to lay a blueprint for where you plan to spend your time, and it can evolve throughout the following day if it needs to. I typically write out a daily schedule list five days a week and give myself the weekend off to allow for free flow time.

Setting Long-Term Goals

It's easy to get wrapped up in daily tasks of running a business and completely forget about setting long-term goals. Long-term goal setting requires getting quiet with yourself and looking toward your business mission statement (Chapter 3), getting clear on your goals, and then incrementally implementing them into your daily schedule.

Everyone sets long-term goals differently, so it's all about doing what works best for you. If you consistently set long-term goals and reflect upon them, you will learn what type of goal setting works best for you.

I like to set long-term goals at the change of every year, around January 1. With the ending of the holiday and quietness of winter in the northern hemisphere, I find this a great time to hunker down with myself and create goals for the year ahead. January 1 is also when the fiscal year rolls over to a clean slate, so it can be a good time to set business financial goals and reflect on my sales from the previous year. Not only do I set business and creativity goals, but I also set financial and personal goals. My business is part of me, but I am not my business. Whenever I am goal setting, it's an all-encompassing event, like taking inventory on my life.

At the beginning of each month, I also like to set smaller goals based on my larger annual goals. If it feels aligned, I like to set intentions at each new moon, though I feel that these intentions are often more internally based than business focused. For the past two years I created my own moon planner, which asks monthly questions and new/full moon questions, providing writing space for reflection and goal setting. I have found this journal process helpful to get clear on where I am headed.

The moral of the story is that whatever type of goal setting works best for you, it's important to spend time on this as an Artist and business owner. It's a way to set your sights on where you want to go.

Balance vs. Burnout

As a Working or Professional Artist, it is hard to balance it all—the creative process, running a business, social media, website, photography, emails, not to mention self-care . . . the to-do list goes on.

There have been times throughout my career, especially in the beginning, that I've burned myself to a crisp and wanted to quit because I felt like "I just can't do it all anymore." The most dramatic burnout hit me during the holiday season of 2018, while I was working out of that second bedroom in the rental. I hadn't taken a weekend off since I went full-time art, over a year before. After my second holiday season of packaging hundreds of orders, I was *over it*.

Yes, I was honored that so many people wanted to own my art. But, I wondered, was this all there was to being an Artist? Being stuck in an eight-by-eight-foot room for ten hours a day, every day? *I wanted freedom.* I craved inspiration. So I convinced Kory to quit his job. We sold most of our belongings, packed our remaining items into a storage unit, and drove our painted van down the West Coast to Los Angeles, where we sold the van. We then boarded a one-way flight to Mexico. Yeah, we were *really* "on one."

It was an epic adventure, that's for sure. In Mexico, we shared a casita with a group of creatives for four weeks, and then we went off on our own adventure to Baja. We had a blast. But I began to find that fun carried me only so far, and I craved a *purpose* to ground into. I attempted to run my business from Mexico, and for a while it worked, but opportunities began to arise back home that I couldn't tend to while I was away.

I began to worry about how I didn't even have an art studio to return to. We had disassembled our lives and bailed. *What had I done?!* After two months, I was homesick for the PNW and an art studio, so we flew home. I definitely don't regret this adventure, and I certainly crave more international escapades. However, now I know that my business always needs a home base, no matter how far away I travel.

I do believe this burnout incident would have been avoidable if I had given myself more breaks during that first year of being a full-time Artist. If I had been easier on myself and acknowledged my hard work, and if I had hired someone to package my orders, maybe I still would have boarded that flight to Mexico while also leaving my art studio intact. Hindsight sure is twenty-twenty.

🌲🌲🌲

Over the years, I've learned that being an Artist is an all-encompassing lifestyle that requires me to care for my body, mind, and spirit. If I don't, my art suffers. *I* suffer. Running a business is hard. Being an Artist is hard. Failures sting and creative block is real. However, the longer time has gone on, the more I ease into trusting the process. All those times I thought about quitting, I am sure glad I didn't.

My dear reader, take it from me: self-care is a *must.*

How do you fill up your tank? We all need time to refuel and collect inspiration. We can't run on empty forever. Are you getting enough sleep? Are you resting and refueling? Exercising? Finding inspiration? Allowing yourself to take a vacation? The sooner you can establish healthy habits and balance in your life and in your career, the better your art will become. And that's what we are going for here—longevity.

A note to those who might be struggling with burnout right now (and a note to my past and future self): allow yourself to take a *break*. Maybe even just for a day. For a week. Hustle culture might tell you that this will kill your business, but it's the other way around. Short-term success does not equal long-term abundance. Your longevity depends on you feeling fueled up and abundant! Your art and business should support *you* living your best life! Not suck your life energy out of you.

CHAPTER 3

The Business

Back when I was a So You Wanna Be, dreaming of becoming an Artist, I had grand romantic visions of what it would be like to be a Professional Artist. There were flowing curtains blowing in a gentle breeze upon my workspace. In professional but painterly attire, I would simply spend the day painting in my tranquil studio, while my paintings flew out the door for thousands of dollars. This is what being a Professional Artist is, right?!

Well, my dear reader, if you have similar grandiose ideas like I did, it's time to burst your bubble. Being a Professional Artist doesn't necessarily mean creating all day, every day. Because if you are *selling* your art, you are also now *running* a business. And it turns out running a business takes a lot of time. The thing is, many of the *business* aspects take place behind the scenes (that is, you don't see them from the outside or through the customer-facing art). This is why I was in for a wake-up call when I made the transition to Professional Artist. Suddenly I was running a freaking business—*whoa!*

Becoming Your Own Boss

Advice I received when I was an Artist striving to become a Working Artist:

"You need to start treating art like your job."

How do I make the jump from creating art to selling art?

So you're an Artist ready to make the jump to Working Artist. Congratulations! You've put in all that hard work to develop your style, you've honed in on your creative process, and you've even created a body of work. Plus, you're owning the fact that you are now an Artist. Time to give yourself a pat on the back! Just getting to this point is a commendable feat in itself.

Before you become a Professional Artist, you need to get things going as a Working Artist. You don't want to put all the financial pressure to support your livelihood on your creativity. This is a recipe for failure. So it is important to have a life situation that allows for backup funds and a second source of income. You also need to get your business systems dialed in as a Working Artist, so that when it comes time to rely solely on your art business for your livelihood, you have systems in place that allow your business to thrive.

Let's start with step one: if you want art to be your job, you must start treating art like your job. And your first task on day one of this job is to legitimize your business.

Making It Legal

Before you start selling any products, or spending any money, you need to establish an LLC and get a business license. If you're already making money and have been putting off getting the legal side dialed in, I am here to tell you, IT'S TIME. *Why?* Because the sooner you do it, the more legitimate your business has the potential to become and the closer you are to becoming a Professional Artist.

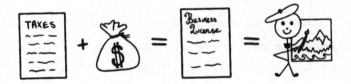

Sure, it sucks to pay taxes on your hard-earned income as an Artist. But there are two facts of life: death and taxes. Taxes are unavoidable. The government wants their share of the pie. The sooner you take care of these logistics, the easier your life will become as a Working Artist.

Over the years I have met Artists selling their work who have yet to apply for a business license or pay taxes on their earnings, even though they are aware they should. My question to these

Artists is: *Do you believe in your art and yourself?* If the answer is yes, it's time to make it legit. If the answer is no, should you really be selling anything at all?

When I began selling my art, I was unaware that I needed to have a business license. Back when I had one foot in the door, working in a restaurant, and one foot out the door, pursuing my art business, I didn't track ANY of my business expenses or income. I figured that since taxes were already being deducted from my paycheck, the government probably didn't care about the measly amount I had made off my art. After all, I barely took myself seriously as an Artist. I was still a So You Wanna Be at this point. Once I made the decision to quit my restaurant job and move into the rental, I knew the time had finally come to get some help with taxes and legal details.

Teetering on my brand-new baby-Professionl-Artist legs, with $8,000 to my name, I walked into an accountant's office in January 2018. I sat at the wooden desk under fluorescent lights, across from my new accountant, whose lined face showed he had been looking at other people's money for a long time.

I explained how I was ready to establish an LLC for my art. He began asking questions. "Did you make money off your art the previous year?"

"Yes."

"Do you know how much?"

"No."

"Did you track any of your expenses?"

"No."

Finally, with a sigh, he said, "I am assuming this means you didn't collect any Washington State sales tax?"

"Nope."

In his crackly but knowledgeable voice, he said, "Oh, wow, you've created a real mess for yourself here, haven't you?"

"Did I?" I asked softly, my palms growing sweaty. Unknown to me at the time of selling my art, the IRS and Washington State were going to want their cut of the income and transactions I had made back in 2017. He instructed me to go home, go through all my bank statements from 2017, and categorize my expenses and income in an Excel spreadsheet. I was also to categorize all the Washington State sales in a separate column by the city of where the sale had occurred. I did what I was told. To my great shock, I found that I had made over $20,000 (!!!) off my art in 2017 and had spent about $5,000 in expenses. This was all news to me.

I sent the Excel sheet to the accountant and a few days later learned that I owed $2,500 in taxes to the federal government and $500 to Washington State for sales tax. Plus there was the $400 bill from the accountant (my bank account went from $8,000 to $4,500 overnight). I immediately burst into tears. It felt like a punch to the gut. I had no idea that it was so expensive to be self-employed, or that the government was somehow entitled to that much of the money that I had made off blood, sweat, tears, and brushstrokes.

But I had no other choice, so I paid my dues. I established an LLC in Washington State and registered for a business license. I opened separate business checking and savings accounts that all my business transactions would run in and out of, streamlining tracking my business transactions. I set up a QuickBooks account, an online bookkeeping tool for businesses. With the help of my accountant, I cleaned up my mess. But the whole shocking scenario could have been avoided if I had legitimized my business before I started making money.

So what's the moral of the story, my little So You Wanna Bes and Artists? *Don't do what I did.* Don't wait until art is your only source of income to become legit. Get the legal stuff taken care of *now.*

Unless you have an accounting background, I would recommend hiring an accountant to help you get started. You already have SO MUCH to do running your own business, and finding an accountant can help alleviate the pressure of taxes. Your accountant should be able to walk you through all the steps below if you need help, which you likely will.

Legitimize Your Art Business Checklist:
- ❏ Hire an accountant.
- ❏ Establish an LLC in your state.
- ❏ Register for a business license.
- ❏ Apply for a reseller license.
- ❏ Open a business checking account.
- ❏ Sign up for QuickBooks.
- ❏ Collect sales tax and file state quarterly taxes.
- ❏ File quarterly federal estimated payments.
- ❏ File annual federal taxes.

The Jobs within the Job

Okay, cool, now that you are legit, let's take a closer look at what it's like to have art be your job. Errr, I mean *jobs*.

There are three main jobs within my art business:

1. Creativity
2. Marketing
3. Business

I compartmentalize these roles, and they are where most of my time is spent daily and weekly. On average, I spend an equal amount of time on each category. So if I work forty hours a week, that means I spend only 13.33 hours painting (it really depends on the week, though, and the particular projects). In the past, I used to work sixty to seventy hours per week, with at least twenty to twenty-five hours of painting on average. But after a while, this lifestyle grew unsustainable for me (reference the "Balance vs. Burnout" section for more). Personally, I need a work–life balance. Especially when starting a business, it's possible and almost expected that you might be working overtime as you dial in all of your systems.

On my computer, I've organized my different jobs as categorized folders and subfolders.

The CREATIVITY Folder:

✌ Painting images: all my pieces from the last eight years

- Product design: mock-ups for products
- Video: all video content, raw and edited (in my brain this lives in Creativity rather than Marketing, because I've always felt that video is part of my creative expression)
- Writing: any blogs, this book

The MARKETING Folder:

- Photos (Instagram and marketing)
- Product photos
- Email campaigns

The BUSINESS Folder:

- Clients
- Subfolders: Brands, Individuals, Wholesale
- LLC details
- Receipts
- Taxes

As you can see, there are a lot of details and time that goes into each job, and until you have enough disposable income to hire help, there will be a lot to do. This is another reason I recommend having an additional source of income, taking your time as a Working Artist to dial in all these systems, and saving money before you become a Professional Artist.

The more your business grows, the more busywork there will be. Eventually, as a Professional Artist, you may need to hire help.

Two years ago I did this, as I was spending way too much time on the back-end tasks of my business. I now employ one part-time employee who fulfills orders, packages prints, and organizes inventory. As the years have gone on, the back-end tasks of my business have grown, and I spend less and less time creating. I am now in a place that I am beginning to hire out additional behind-the-scenes roles to assist my business's growth, and so I can spend more time creating and making art. In fact, there are more aspects of delegating than I have room to elaborate on here. . . I guess I'll have to save them for my next book!

When I began selling my art, I had a part-time job serving tables, plus a catering gig on the side, and I was living with my parents rent-free. I was fortunate to have a supportive family who encouraged me to strive to become a Professional Artist. I painted in the mornings and late nights after my shifts. After a while, I realized the late-night hours at the restaurant, not to mention the slightly toxic environment, were damaging my self-care and thus making it impossible for me to succeed as an up-and-coming Artist. Plus, I was painting in the corner of my parents' living room.

My art was in high demand, and I could barely keep up with the Instagram messages and order requests that were coming in, all while I was also working two other jobs. Some days I spent all day before work tracking down the right box to fit a painting, then packaging and shipping out the painting, just in time to clock into my night job. How the heck was I supposed to paint and manage sales at the same time? Being a Working Artist is a *hard* act to balance. So, after saving up enough money that last summer to cover a few months' living expenses, I quit my service industry jobs and moved into a two-bedroom rental several hours from my parents' house.

At the age of twenty-three, I made the transition to Professional Artist at a time in my life when I had very little responsibility. I had some savings. Plus I had a backup plan—bartending—if all else failed. But I still had a lot to learn. Fresh out of college, I was in for a wake-up call. I had never worked a full-time job, and suddenly every day was spent alone in my rental far away from friends and family, trying to figure out how to turn my dream into a reality. It got lonely at times. It got overwhelming. I knew nothing about running a business, and suddenly there I was running one.

As you can imagine, I did not have all my systems dialed in before making this transition. My e-commerce website was subpar, I handwrote addresses on orders, and I did not have an LLC established. But on the flip side, my Instagram audience was growing, and projects seemed to be flowing my way. People were messaging me, asking to buy my art before it was posted for sale on my website. Ultimately it all worked out. But that's not to say it wasn't a bumpy start.

My point is that there is no right or wrong way to make the transition in your life from a Working Artist to a Professional Artist. But there is definitely a way to make it more *easeful*. If I could go back, there are things I would change about how I made this transition, but here we are again—hindsight is twenty-twenty. Hopefully you can learn from my story, use what resonates, and apply it to your own life. With any luck, this will help you be a tad more set up than I was.

Creating Your Own Little Universe

One of the most empowering parts of starting a business is that YOU get to set the business's universal laws. It's your little universe, after all. What do I mean by universal laws? Well, here on earth, we are governed by the law of gravity. Now it's your turn to create something akin to gravity. It's your business. **You make the rules.** It's your job to create the container (universe) in which your business can grow—heck, *thrive*. The clearer you can become on the *why* behind your business, the stronger your business will become.

Thanks to the help of my business coach Jen,[4] I created my business mission statement and defined my core values before I had even established my LLC. This was such an important step in bringing the business to life—it laid the foundation for what I was building. It helped me see the potential in my mission to share my art and story with the world.

Mission Statement

From the get-go, it is important to set a clear intention for your business's North Star. This will help create your business mission

---

4 CADENCE COACHING at jenverharen.com.

statement. Over the years, my mission statement has helped me stay aligned with my *why* and to remember who I am serving and how. It is helpful to use in marketing purposes, bios, and brand messaging (we will cover marketing in Chapter 6). And it is essential when I am making business decisions.

🌲🌲🌲

North Star and Mission Worksheet

1. *What* is your business bringing to the world?

2. *How* is your business bringing your *what* to the world?

3. *Why* is your business bringing this to the world?

Once you know your *what, how* and *why*, you can set goals based on your answers. This North Star will also help you in the future if you get knocked off track.

For example, here is my North Star:

1. What is your art business bringing to the world? *My art and my story.*
2. How is your business bringing your *what* to the world? *Through sharing (that is, storytelling and visually showing my art in public and on the internet).*
3. Why is your business bringing this to the world? *To inspire others to realize their dreams, even when they seem out of reach.*

From here, you can create your mission statement.

My mission statement:
By sharing my art and story with the world, I hope to inspire others to realize their dreams, even when they seem out of reach.

Your mission statement:

So You Wanna Be an Artist?

Core Values Worksheet

Next, define your core values: a set of three to five values. These will act as a moral compass for your art business. Your core values help you make decisions and further develop your business. They can guide you in the right direction, decide whether an opportunity is a yes or no, and even aid in deciding what products to create (more on this in Chapter 4).

My Art Business's Core Values:

1. Make the world a better place.
2. Make earth-friendly choices.
3. Create and consume consciously.
4. Inspire others to be the best version of themselves.

Your core values don't need to be complicated; in fact, you probably already know them just from being a human and living life on this planet! Now it's time to write them out.

Your Core Values:

1.
2.
3.
4.
5.

60

🌲🌲🌲

Your Relationship with Money

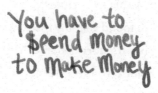

Back when I had one foot in the door with art and one foot out the door at a restaurant, I received some solid-gold advice: "You have to spend money to make money." You see, I was afraid to invest in my art, because I had only a couple thousand dollars in the bank at the time, and spending it on something I wasn't sure I was going to make back felt really scary.

Here's a sweet little secret: *you're never going to know if it's going to work until you try.* Even now, when I invest in bringing a new product into my online store, I don't know if it's going to sell. Because in business, until it hits the market, no matter how businesslike you want to get about it, you still won't know if it will sell until you get real-time sales from your customers.

And here's another little trade secret: the most successful people in the world take **risks**. Risks with their finances, with their time, with their energy. They stick their neck out with an idea and figure out how to make it work. Take Steve Jobs. No one knew what

Apple or the iPhone was until he invented it. Heck, no one knew they needed an iPhone, and now we literally can't seem to survive without them. Sure, taking a big risk also has great potential for failure. You *could* lose everything you invest. Or you *could* sell out and make a profit. So it's important to practice calculated risk-taking (we will cover more of this in Chapter 4).

Over the years I've found that my relationship with money has more to do with my brain's story about it than the actual reality of the number in my bank accounts.[5] Money is essential to sustaining our basic needs (food, water, shelter), so it is easy to have our relationship with it be based on survival mode. However, money can also be a tool to grow, expand, and receive abundance. Let me explain . . .

I remember the first time I spent money on my business, other than buying art supplies from the art store. I spent $300 on bulk packaging supplies, and my brain felt as though it was going to DIE. Three hundred dollars is A LOT of groceries, after all.

You see, when I opened my online store, I had prints, stickers, and originals for sale. I began getting orders right away. Every time I sold something, I went to the post office to buy a padded mailer to ship it out. If you didn't know this already, buying individual mailers at the post office is a lot more expensive per unit than buying them in bulk online. But the up-front cost of buying one mailer (~$3.50) versus 250 (~$300) is obviously lower. And I found

---

5 Ramit Sethi's book *I Will Teach You to Be Rich* talks a lot about this. I highly recommend reading his book and checking out his podcast.

this shift difficult to wrap my mind around because of the way I related to my money. It took me months to grasp the fact that if I spent more money at once buying in bulk, I would actually *save* money in the long run.

Money = Time

I eventually realized that not only was I spending a ridiculous amount on individual mailers from the post office, but I was spending my *time* waiting in line to buy them. If I wanted my business to grow, I needed to stop waiting in line daily at the post office. This realization required that I move out of survival mode, recognize that my art was selling, and trust that it would continue to sell. Over time, I have shifted how I view money—it's a *tool*, not a jewel. If you want your business to work, you are going to have to spend money.

How do I know when I am ready to sell my art?

Ready to Sell My Art Checklist:
- ❒ You are an Artist.
- ❒ You have genuine interest in selling your art.
- ❒ You have an established LLC and business license.
- ❒ You have defined your mission statement and core values.
- ❒ You are ready to invest in your art business.

CHAPTER 4

The Products

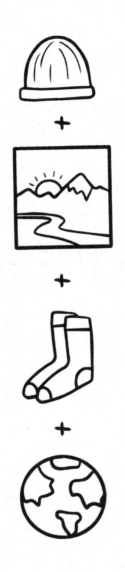

Okay, now that we've established you need to spend money on your business for your business to make money, it's time to decide what you'll spend your money on. The good news is that there are many ways to make money off your art. It's all about being creative and following your curiosity. Thus far in my career the *primary* way I have gone about making money is by selling products.

By *products*, I am referring to the following:

1. Originals
2. Fine art prints
3. Merch (stickers, apparel, hats, planners, notebooks, calendars, etc.)

Calculated Risk-Taking

If you are just budding as a Working Artist, I would recommend you start off small and simple with products. Slow and steady wins this race. You don't want to spend all your savings on products and then sell only half the product while the other half sits there (and meanwhile you are running out of funds). This is where it becomes extremely important to make calculated risks so that you don't bankrupt yourself in the process of investing and selling product.

When I began selling products over the internet, I didn't have much capital to invest in creating products, so I was limited in what products I could sell. I focused on selling my originals, stickers, and prints. Simple and straightforward. And even though my business has grown over the years, I still choose to keep my product line limited, as this aligns with my core values.

How do you use calculated risk-taking?

Invest no more than 20 percent of what you have in your bank account into product, then sell it. Use the profit to purchase more product to sell, again, 20 percent of what you have. Repeat this pattern. If your products sell successfully (that is, you are able to sell out of or most of your product), over time you will make a profit you can use to grow your business.

Why invest only 20 percent?

The goal here is longevity, and it's best not to put yourself in a position in which you are overly exposed financially. According to Ramit Sethi,[6] it's best to have at least six months of living expenses in your bank account in case of emergency. It's important to be smart when starting a business. Depending on your situation and responsibilities, you may be able to invest a larger or smaller percentage, but 20 percent feels like a safe percentage in my humble opinion.

For you, 20 percent might mean you start with a $200 initial investment in stickers. Next, reinvest those profits. *Build from where you are instead of focusing on where you aren't.*

Order Fulfillment

When you begin accumulating products and shipping supplies, you'll need to expand your physical workspace. I would recommend you compartmentalize—keep your creative space for creating and, if possible, set up a separate table for your business space.

Little did I realize when I started out that running an online business selling fragile paintings over the internet meant that I was on the road to becoming a packaging professional. Over the past five years, I've gone from needing my stepdad to help me build a box for my first painting I sold online to now having an entire section of my studio dedicated to packaging products. The more you package, the easier it gets. If you plan to sell products over the internet, then you, my friend, will also become a packaging professional.

---

6 Sethi, Ramit, *I Will Teach You to Be Rich* (New York: Workman Publishing, 2009).

Remember back when I was standing in line at the post office to buy those padded mailers? Well, to add to my inefficiency, I was also handwriting each recipient's mailing address and manually entering tracking numbers into the computer. There were some days where I spent *hours* just addressing packages. I didn't know any better. Finally I switched my website host to Shopify, which offered an integrated order-fulfillment system that allowed me to purchase and print labels from my studio. This automated the whole ordeal and saved me hours. I've found this is often how systems in my business evolve . . . they start out super inefficient and eventually become more streamlined. Suddenly something that used to take hours now takes minutes. It's constant learning over here, my friends.

Okay, now let's get into what you came here for . . . you want to start a business, so what is your business gonna sell, my little Artists? We are about to get to the juicy stuff.

Originals

Depending on what type of art you create, your originals may be your most **important** product.

As a painter, this is true for me. My originals are the **meat** of my business. Not only do originals require a lower overhead and offer higher profit margins than other products, but they also hold value. They are one of a kind. Plus, I reproduce my original designs on products. I license my original designs to companies.

I create high-quality prints of my originals . . . the possibilities are endless.

It's important to get **high-quality photographs** of your originals before they sell so that you can continue using the design for years to come. I work with a local fine art photographer who photographs my originals and makes my prints.

In the past, I have sold originals without first retaining a high-quality photograph of them. I always regret this later. Once a piece is sold, it's almost impossible to get that high-resolution image you need, especially when the piece has been shipped to a different state. Don't do what I did! Get your originals photographed right when you finish them.

How do you price your originals?

My pricing ranges from $500 to $5,000 per original, based on size, detail, and value. I price my originals based on how I *feel* about the piece. This might sound like silly logic, but it works for me. If I absolutely love the work I created, I will price it higher than something I am not as excited about. This is the *value* piece of the pricing equation. Next I factor in time and size.

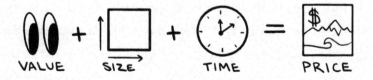

VALUE + SIZE + TIME = PRICE

Price your originals *higher* than you think you should. If you've already sold originals for less than you should have, that's okay. But I'm here to tell you to **charge more**. Your originals are *unique*. When you first start selling your work, you might want to begin your pricing a bit lower, but once you find there's a demand, raise your prices.

Originals shouldn't be flying off the shelf once a day. Since you are spending **quality** time on your art, as I know you are, you likely won't be producing an original once a day. At least, I definitely don't do that. Originals take thought from the creator, so purchasing one should also take thought from the buyer. *These are not impulse-buy items.* **They are valuable investments.** And their price should reflect this. My originals are designer items. And I am constantly working to raise my pricing.

Finally, if you price your originals low, you are not only doing a disservice to yourself but to all Artists out there who sell their art. Once your art is posted for sale, it enters the marketplace and influences the industry standard of art sales. The way you price your art influences buyers' expectations of not just you, but *all* Artists. Do yourself and all of us Working/Professional Artists a favor and price your work with the quality it deserves.

I sold my second original to a customer on the internet who contacted me through DM (direct messaging on Instagram) for $450 (the first painting I sold was to Rachel Pohl, so I asked for the same price for the second piece, as it was the only reference point I had). *I was ecstatic.* I could barely believe a stranger wanted to purchase my art! To me, as a Working Artist, $450 was not only a lot of money, *but a lot of money for someone to pay for my art.* It was an amazing feeling.

Since that sale, I've significantly raised my pricing for several reasons, the first being that there is proven demand for my originals, so I can charge more because the market will pay more. Second, now that I am a Professional Artist, I've been hit with the reality of how much it *costs* to run a business, so my pricing must cover my costs. And if I sold every original for $450, I would definitely not be covering my costs. Third, originals take a large time investment; plus they are valuable and one of a kind, so they get a high price point. As I've grown as a Professional Artist both in skill and reputation, the price of my originals has risen. As you grow as a Working and Professional Artist, *raise your pricing!*

PS: *Don't forget to sign your originals!*

Note about Copyrights

As the sole creator of your original designs, you retain the sole copyrights. Even when you sell a physical artwork (unless it is otherwise stated in writing and signed by you), you retain the copyrights. As an Artist, your original designs are your assets. **Never sell your copyrights.** You retain the right to reproduce the design however you please even after the physical original has sold, unless someone has *licensed* the right to reproduce your design as stated in a licensing agreement (more on this in the "Licensing" section).

Commissions

What is a commission?

A commission is the act of hiring an Artist to create a work based on the client's request.

Commissions also fall under our "Originals" category. Though the subject matter may be directed by the client, a commission is still an original piece and should be treated as such—as in, the commission should hold true to your unique style and core values.

Early on, while I was still ironing out my commission process, I had a client ask me to use another Artist's work as a reference image for the commission piece. I respectfully walked away from the prospective project because that would be *copying*, and a true Artist never copies, right? Remember, this is your little universe, and you make the rules, **especially** when working with clients. It's always okay to say "No, thank you" to a project. In fact, I say "No, thank you" quite often, so that I can say "Hell yes!" when an opportunity arises that I am really interested in.

Throughout my career, I have picked up commission projects here and there, but I do tend to get burned out on working creatively with client requests. For me, creating art is all about moment-to-moment inspiration, and I've found working on commissions can feel forced. So I learned quickly that I needed to be highly selective with the type of commission projects I accept. I like to have as much creative freedom as possible in my process. I have never advertised my commission services and have accepted only select commissions that come my way. To weed out serious commission clients from the less serious, I state up front to the client that my commission minimum is $1,500 before we get on the phone to discuss the commission. If I entertained every commission request that came into my inbox before stating my minimum, I would be on the phone all day. Serious buyers only, please.

My best advice for you regarding commissions? Try one or two projects and see how you like them. You'll likely come up on some road bumps, but you can iron out your commission process if you enjoy this type of work.

I have heard from a few Artists that they get burned out when they take on too many commissions at once. Working on a commission means that you are not only creating an original but working with a client, which takes extra time and energy. If you don't have a clear client communication going in, it's easy to get overwhelmed. Be highly selective with the commission projects you accept and which clients you choose to work with.

When working with a client, it is important to maintain clear communications and manage client expectations:

1. Don't make any promises to a potential client until you are 100 percent certain that you want to work with them.
2. Be firm on your pricing and communicate your rate before doing any work.
3. Charge at least a 50 percent up-front deposit (receiving a

partial payment before you begin any work helps to ensure you're working with a reliable client).

4. Communicate all important aspects that will be in the **commission agreement** verbally so that both parties are on the same page.

5. Set a clear timeline of when the client should expect to receive a creation update and the final product.

Commission Process Checklist:

❐ State commission minimum.

❐ Schedule a "vision call" with client.

❐ During vision call:

   ❐ Get a feel for client's personality and style.

   ❐ Discuss desired subject matter, colors, and favorite works that you've created.

❐ Send follow-up email with the commission fee and commission agreement.[7]

❐ Retain 50 percent nonrefundable deposit and signed commission agreement.

❐ Create sketch one (I digitally render my sketches) and send to client for approval.

❐ Once client approves sketch, begin creation process.

❐ Enjoy the fun part: creation time!

❐ Update client on creation process.

---

7 I created my own commission agreement with the help of online templates and a lawyer. Basically, you want the agreement to spell out the terms of the agreement, including project start and end dates and fees.

❐ Send photo of final piece and invoice final payment.

❐ Receive final payment.

❐ Deliver final piece.

Commission Agreements

If I am working with an individual client (versus a company), my commission agreement is brief and straight to the point. It spells out expectations for the project in writing so that we have a reference in case something goes sideways.

During a vision call, I discuss my commission process, including all important details that go into the commission agreement. One of the most important notes I verbally state to every client is that I retain the copyrights to my work, including my right to reproduce the design. When I am working with a private client who wants to hang the commission in their home, this contingency has never been a hang-up. There are times when a client wants to use and reproduce the design for business purposes, and in these cases, we include a licensing agreement into the contract (see licensing information that follows). Licensing adds to the total cost of the project.

There are helpful templates online that you can use to form your own commission template; however, I always recommend seeking professional legal advice for anything signed in writing.

Commission Agreement Checklist:

- ❐ Project name.
- ❐ Start and end dates.
- ❐ Project overview.
- ❐ Project timeline with dates.
- ❐ Payment terms.
- ❐ Copyright notice.
- ❐ Signatures of both parties.

Fine Art Prints

Fine art prints are created by capturing a high-resolution photograph of an original and then using the giclée fine art printing process to make the prints. Next, prints are made using the giclée printing process, which is UV resistant and maintains color for hundreds of years.

I have been selling some of the same print designs for five-plus years, and they keep selling. *See?* Your original designs are not only valuable but also *maintain* their value. And because your prints are high-value items, they should be created using a high-quality printing process by a professional.

How do I find a professional fine art printer to make prints?
Search for someone in your area who photographs fine art and can make fine art prints with the giclée printing process, especially if your work includes color. Get on the age-old interwebs and google

it! Call around. I promise there is a professional print maker out there ready to help you make professional prints.

I get my prints made locally by a fine art photographer. For years I packaged my own fine art prints by hand (I trimmed down the edges, cut out the mat backing, and slipped them into a clear sleeve). Now I have a lovely employee who takes care of this for me, but the production line still takes place in my studio.

I would not recommend using a basic print shop for your prints, and I especially do not recommend making prints from a home printer, as these will be lower quality and will likely not be a good representation of your art. Cheap ink fades quickly. It's giclée all the way.

Sign your prints! Adding your signature mark makes them more valuable, especially as you begin to build a reputation.

Pricing

My print pricing ranges from $35 to $100 for regular sizing (the prints packed flat with backing), and I offer XL print sizing that requires the prints be shipped rolled in a cardboard tube, with pricing ranging from $200 to $400.

Merchandise

My definition of merchandise (merch) includes anything that is not handmade by you, the Artist (prints are technically signed, so I do not categorize these as merch). Merch includes products such as stickers, hats, apparel, and notebooks.

I typically release a limited selection of merch a couple of times a year. My highest sales period is always before the holidays, so I create and release the most products of the year during this time. I like to keep merch limited and focus on creating goods that I love and use in my daily life so that I can confidently market and represent them to my audience.

Profit Margins

Profit margins on merch (like stickers) and printed goods (like greeting cards) are generally pretty good. If it costs one dollar to make a sticker, and it is sold for five dollars. That's a 500 percent markup, which is a great profit margin, especially if sold in higher quantities.

Profit margins on soft goods like hats and apparel are not as great, especially when ordering in small batches. Minimum order quantities are usually high, but the more you order, the lower the per-unit price. Most hat companies I've worked with have a minimum of fifty hats per order, and minimums with apparel can vary.

Example 1: You purchase forty-eight hats at a unit price of $12.83 each. That's $615.84 total, plus $40 in freight. Let's say you sell these hats at $30 per unit. You need to sell twenty-one hats to break even. Once you break even, your total profit margin is $824.16 if you sell these hats at full price with no discounts.

Example 2: Let's say I make a T-shirt. It costs $8 to make this tee, so I double it for my wholesale price, meaning a wholesaler would pay $16 for it, and it would retail for $32. To get the MSRP value, I triple my cost. The higher markup, the more money I make.

Creating and ordering merchandise takes time, so it's important to make sure the demand for that product is there (reference "Calculated Risk-Taking"!). I have found that in our current economy, it costs even more to make earth-friendly things. Remember: simple, slow, and steady wins this race!

How do I know what merchandise will sell?

You won't know how successful a merch product is until it hits the market. Sure, you can poll your audience and look around at what others are selling. But as far as converting opinions to actual sales, I find it's a bit of a guessing game. Merch that I've thought would move slower has flown off the shelf, and merch I've been super excited about has moved slowly. Not to mention that merch that sits there unsold is essentially a sunk cost.

Selling out of a merch product you envisioned and brought into production is a great feeling. The payout can also be substantial. If you take your time in building out your merchandise line, you are much more likely to be successful.

How to Start a Merchandise Line:

- Select a few designs from your body of work.
- Create two to five products with those designs.
- Order in small quantities to start.

❧ Introduce only a few products (that you really love) at
a time.

❧ See what sells best and what doesn't.

❧ Make more of what sells.

How to Get Your Art on Merch

As I discussed above, I have a fine art photographer who photographs my art and makes my prints. After capturing a high-res
photo, he sends me the file. From here, my art is digitized, and I
can reproduce it onto almost anything.

However, there is a difference between a JPEG/PDF file
and the vector/CMYK files that are used to print most apparel,
mugs, and other products.[8] I am not going to bore you with all
the printing technicalities, but I'll say this: we live in a time of
overabundance of material. If there is something you want to
put your art on, the answer is yes. You can make virtually any
product with your art on it. You just need to do the heavy lifting
of researching and finding the manufacturer who can meet your
needs. Remember, you're a business owner now, so you have the
power to make professional connections. Don't be afraid to keep
asking questions!

---

8 Hire a graphic designer to help with all of this. Upwork is a fantastic marketplace to
find talent.

Aligning Products with Core Values

It's time to circle back to your core values (see Chapter 3). It's your responsibility as a business owner to ensure your products are aligned with your core values, mission statement, and who you are as an Artist.

Personally, I've always had an internal struggle with manufacturing products, because I don't believe the world needs a bunch more *stuff*. By stuff, I am not referring to my original paintings or fine art prints, because I view these in a separate category from merch; plus the world needs art. By stuff I mean items you buy at a typical store—things such as hats and apparel, anything that is mass manufactured, made in a factory, either in the US or overseas. Anything that I don't make with my own hands.

Two of my core values are "make earth-friendly choices" and "create and consume consciously." So, to align with these values, I do my absolute best to make products as eco-friendly as possible and to produce them in small batches and limited quantities. When I update my website with new products, you may notice that I offer only a few different products at a time. *This is intentional.* I don't want to be a seller of stuff. I want to be a creator of art, in turn "making the world a better place" (another core value).

As a budding Professional Artist and business owner, it can be tricky to stick to your core values, especially when it can cost *way* more to do so. For example, I had my art printed on apparel that was made from non-earth-friendly materials. I knew there were more eco-friendly options out there, but at the time I couldn't justify the extra cost. Plus, I was trying to meet the MSRPs at which a few of my wholesalers were willing to sell the shirts. However, after a few print runs of this apparel, I have since switched to 100 percent cotton/organic cotton tees, because I realized that staying aligned with my core values is more important than saving a few hundred bucks and making a few hundred more. So I took this experience as a lesson to ground into my values. It's okay to stray from your values—it happens. I guarantee every business owner has done so at some point or other. Your core values are there to guide you back. PS: If you haven't done so already, here's a friendly reminder to lay out your core values *before* creating product!

It's a fine line to walk in our world of mass consumerism and material abundance. Earth-friendly items don't necessarily pay out financially in this economy. Through trial and error, I've learned that just because I *can* put my art on any product and it would likely sell doesn't mean I *should*. I believe we all have a responsibility to the integrity and future of our planet and our people, so I do my best to stay aligned with this service. Beyond that, I believe the right customer base will find me based on the quality of work I create. Plus, staying aligned with my core values in the products I create naturally attracts customers who share similar values.

Brand Collaborations

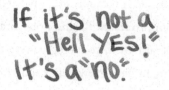

If it's not a
"Hell YES!"
It's a "no".

Besides making your own products, another way to make money off your art is by working with brands that want to use your designs on their products. Brands are always looking for creative ways to market, sell, and design their products.

Connecting with Brands

Brands are much more likely to be interested in working with Artists who have a defined style and a reputation on social media. But most importantly in the world of business, it's not about what you know but who you know. Networking is key in the world of business deals, so strategically positioning yourself within a niche industry is essential if you want to work with brands in such industry.

Most of the brands I've connected with in my career have either been through a referral or meeting the right person in the right place at the right time. Rarely have I worked with a brand that cold emails me straight to my inbox—or vice versa. The best brand deals I've worked on have been through connections to people working within those brands. Business is ultimately a game of human connection, so it's important to prioritize these relationships.

When I first began working with brands, I was extremely

intimidated. But I've learned that behind brands are people who are just as human as me. It's important to be yourself and focus on clear communication. In the right situations, brand collaborations can offer great exposure by introducing your work to a whole new audience; plus they can help grow your reputation as an Artist.

Toward the beginning of my career, I entered a brand deal with a client where clear expectations were not transparently established from the get-go. Looking back with several years of experience, I take full responsibility for the decline of this brand deal. But at the time I was completely gutted. The project scope entailed a series of five paintings that would be used for a sprinter van wrap. In our initial conversations, the client had expressed to me they were interested in licensing the designs for branded merchandise, but we decided to iron out the licensing details later on. This was my first mistake.

The initial contract stated that the five originals would be given to the brand, in addition to the license for a single sprinter van wrap, and that an additional separate licensing contract was required for additional licensing use. When I laid the foundation at the beginning of the project, I should have collected more information on *what* my client was looking for regarding additional licensing and spelled this out in our *initial* contract, instead of leaving it hanging, since this secondary contract would require additional negotiations (as contracts usually do).

Once the painting process was complete, the client wanted to see a "return" on their investment in the paintings by creating merchandise from the paintings. So I sent over a drafted licensing agreement, but the client did not like the terms I had spelled out, and we suddenly hit a roadblock in our communication.

We could not agree on several aspects of the licensing agreement. After three months between the signing of our first contract and the completion of the paintings, I had failed to *manage the expectations* of my client. The client had built expectations for the licensing deal that I was not equipped for. They blamed me for taking advantage of them. I, too, felt taken advantage of. Suddenly this exciting opportunity that I had spent months dedicating my time and energy to had crumbled into a nightmare.

Looking back, I see where I went wrong, but at the time, I was confused at how things had gone so south. I now see I didn't do my due diligence in the beginning by collecting all the information I needed to effectively manage my client's expectations. I also didn't clarify what was possible with a licensing agreement from the start of this relationship. There was just so much I didn't know back then. It was the first huge failure of my career.

This whole situation pushed me in a completely different direction. I didn't want to work with brands ever again. I didn't want to sign any contracts. I just wanted to focus on building my own brand and reputation. In some ways, it fueled my fire to work solely on Gianna Andrews Art. And boy did I work hard. But I eventually realized the mistakes I had made and was able to take it as a lesson.

If I wanted to scale as an Artist, I couldn't do it alone. I began to cautiously open myself up again to brand collaborations.

Working with Brands

When you begin working with a brand, it's important to be clear with your deliverables, manage your client's expectations, and prioritize solid communication throughout the project. Take it from me—it's important to lay out the entire scope of the project from the beginning so that you are on the same page throughout the duration of the project.

Brands are on a budget. In many of my conversations with brands, they negotiate my price down to fit their budget. Walking into your initial conversation with a price in mind will help you determine if the project is right for you. You don't want to start negotiations for a project without being clear with yourself *first* on how much you want to charge. Once you say a number out loud in conversation, it's almost impossible to backpedal for a higher price.

It's best to start high with pricing and negotiate down. I have had several brands try to negotiate a lower price by suggesting the marketing exposure I will receive from the brand deal should compensate for a portion of payment. Though the marketing exposure may be significant, I am a Professional Artist, and *I do not work for free*, so I navigate these types of conversations carefully. Typically I give a 15 percent discount off my original price for any such promotions, and that's only if they seem significant. Also, it's important to get any such marketing trade spelled out in writing (in your contract) to ensure the brand follows through on their end of the deal.

I've worked with brands in a variety of ways over the years, from licensing my art designs to live painting at events to sponsored posting on social media. No matter the subject matter of the brand deal, the formula is generally the same. Follow the brand checklist below and revise as needed!

Working with Brands Checklist:
- ❏ Conduct initial contact call discussing scope of work.
- ❏ Follow up with your price in an email.
- ❏ Agree on price.
- ❏ Revise contract terms.
- ❏ Agree on contract terms.
- ❏ Sign contract.
- ❏ Fulfill deliverables.
- ❏ Get paid.

Licensing

Think of licensing an artwork design as renting a car. The renter gets to drive the car where they want for a certain amount of time, but at the end of their trip, they return the car to the rental company, which owns the car.

Licensing a design to a company means that you allow them to use your design on agreed-upon subject matter (marketing purposes, products, etc.) for an agreed-upon amount of time. Your designs are your assets—they can bring you income for decades to come. If you sell the copyright, you sell the asset. As an Artist, you should never sell the copyrights to your designs. Instead, licensing is a great option that allows you to essentially loan your assets to brands.

Contracts

Get it in writing!

The details of the licensing agreement should be spelled out in a contract that both parties agree upon and sign. Smaller brands may not have a standardized contract that they use, in which case I use my own contract I've developed from a combination of online resources and edits from my attorney. Larger companies have their own legal team and thus their own contracts they prefer to use.

It's very important to be aware of what you are signing when working with brands. Unless you have a legal background, contractual language is dense and not written for the average Artist—or the average human, for that matter. I would highly recommend hiring an attorney to help you develop your own contract or look over a contract BEFORE you sign it, *especially* when you are just starting out. Working with an attorney is pricey, but your art is a *valuable* asset, so that means you need to charge appropriately for licensing. My attorney charges $450 per hour. Typically we communicate via email, and they don't spend more than an hour or two per contract.

When working with a larger brand on the contract process, I request the contract in a Word doc, even if they initially send it in PDF format. This way both my attorney and I can make changes/revisions in the document and send them back to the brand. It is typical to have several rounds of edits, with back-and-forth between both parties, before reaching a consensus and signing.

In my experience, not only will having an attorney make your brand appear more legitimate, but it will also help ensure you are protecting your assets—your art! Before I hired an attorney to review my contracts, a brand once sent me a contract and said to me, "Don't let the legal stuff scare you. Just sign it!" So I did. I have since learned that whether you let the legal stuff "scare" you or not, a contract is a legally binding agreement. It's best to have your ducks in a row before you sign.

Key elements of an art licensing contract include the following:

- *Usage:* What type of license do they get? Exclusive license (only the company can use the design) or nonexclusive license (you can license the design to other companies)?
- *Payment:* When is the payment due and how will it be paid? Companies typically pay either a flat fee for a design or a royalty fee based on the amount of units sold.

- *Term:* the amount of time the brand has the art license.
- *Territory:* locations where the license may be used by the company (web and social media, USA, worldwide, etc.).
- *Additional clauses:* make sure that all promises are spelled out in writing (Did they offer you marketing exposure?).
- *Signature:* it's not a done deal until it's signed by both parties.

Throughout my career, I have had several licensing negotiations with brands that did not end up going through. I have also had several successful licensing deals. It just depends on what the company is looking for and if they can offer you a good price and a fair contract.

✦ ✦ ✦

A while back, I signed a licensing contract with a company for an unlimited amount of designs (I sent them new artwork files as I finished my work). This entailed complicated payment terms of zero payment for the first year and then a 7 percent royalty to be paid out quarterly beginning the second year, a three-year term, and a worldwide license, with exclusivity that these designs could not be printed on a competitor's product. The company promised me (verbally) that this collaboration would also offer me significant brand exposure (which was not spelled out in the contract).

During the three-year term, I was paid out only twice, and that was after requesting to see sales data and receive my royalty payments (if the company had upheld their end of the deal, I would have received eight payments total). On top of that, after the three-year term had expired, the company offered me a new contract for a flat fee of $800 for four designs for another three-year term. I came back with a counteroffer of $3,000, as that's around what I had been paid by this company in the previous three years' sales.

They declined, countering that if I stayed with their brand, they would continue offering me brand exposure as they grow. But here's the thing—if it's not in writing, and the terms are not specifically laid out on what this "brand exposure" means, then it has the potential to be an empty promise. I respectfully declined this offer.

Pricing an Art License

In my experience, it takes confidence and knowing your worth as an Artist to ask a brand for a fair payment and fair terms. I've set my licensing fees based on trial and error—I've been underpaid for licensing deals, so I've worked up my confidence to ask for more. My current beginning rate for the average company: one existing design with a nonexclusive license and a three-year term is $3,500. Exclusivity, new designs, and other clauses can affect the price.

Pro Tip: Be realistic with yourself about how much time and energy the contract requires from you. Think about what number would make you *feel great* about the licensing deal. Next, write this number down and don't stray from it during negotiations.

Live Painting

Live painting is a visual presentation where an Artist creates their art in front of a group or audience. When I live paint, I bring my painting supplies and an easel to an event, set up a mini creative space, and create my art on the scene. Usually I bring a painting that I've already spent a couple of hours on so that I have my initial layers down and I don't have to conceptualize on the spot.

I have live painted at a variety of events, and it is always successful, because people love to see art created in person. It provides an attraction and experience for customers. One of my favorite live-painting events was with 10 Barrel Brewing. They hired me to live paint on their summer beer tour at an outdoor location in Seattle. I set up a merch table so that I could sell my art, and I had a friend run sales so that I could focus on painting. The painting I created was then raffled off online, and the proceeds went to charity. The brand compensated me for the price of the painting, and I also received great exposure, as this event drew in a crowd.

Sponsored Social Media Posts

After six years of growing my social media following and presence through art, only in the past year have I worked on sponsored social media posts (save a select project a few years back). Yes, sponsored social media posts can be a nice way to make a supplemental income, but it is my goal that they do not diminish the art brand that I have so carefully crafted. I am highly selective on which brands I choose to work with, and I've done my best to incorporate my art and self as authentically as possible into such posts.

Since this is a book on becoming an Artist, I am not going to delve deep into sponsored social media posts other than to say that it's important to be highly selective of brands you work with in order to maintain the integrity of your brand. If you find a brand that allows you to be you, and shares similar core values with your business, a collaboration can be a great thing.

To work with brands via digital marketing, you first need to build an established online presence and following (more on this in Chapter 6). For me, it was never the main objective to advertise for any brand other than my own via social media. Instead, it's been something that has become aligned with my brand as I've grown my audience.

CHAPTER 5

Commerce

The more diversity you have in your business, the better.

Income Streams

As a Working Artist striving to become a Professional Artist, it's time to get clear on your income streams. The more income streams you have consistently depositing money into your bank account, the more resilient your business will become. Once you have solid income streams established, it will be easier to become a Professional Artist. We will cover two categories of income streams:

1. Business to Consumer (B2C)—selling directly to a customer.
2. Business to Business (B2B)—selling directly to a business.

My favorite part about being a self-employed Artist is not only that I get to be creative with my art, but also that *I get to be creative with the ways in which I make money.* I've dabbled with a lot of ways to make an income off my art. When I am burned out on one income stream, I shift my focus to another income stream. For example, I closed my online e-commerce store for five months during 2022, and my business continued to thrive. The truth is that there are a lot of ways to make money in this world. Once you realize this potential, income streams might open up in areas you don't expect. Remember, there is no right or wrong way to set up your income streams. Craft them however best fits your life as an Artist.

We will cover the following income streams:

1. Online sales
2. Gallery consignment
3. Wholesale
4. Licensing
5. Events

Let's run through all the income streams that support my business and look at the pros and cons of each.

Online Sales

Pros	Cons
• It's inexpensive to open an online store (my monthly subscription fee for Shopify is $30 per month).	• There's a lot of competition on the internet. How will you stand out?
• Less infrastructure is needed (you don't need a storefront).	• You need space to store packaging materials and backstock . . . this could be an issue if you are already tight on space.
• You can open and run the store from anywhere, anytime.	• Packaging orders is time consuming.
• You keep 100 percent of the profits, aside from the credit card processing fee.	• There is a ~2.9 percent credit card processing fee, and these companies often raise their fees.
• The store is open 24/7.	• You need to ship orders promptly (within one to two days of order placement).
• You don't need to hire employees to run the floor.	

A Note on Print-on-Demand Services

Print-on-demand services (like Redbubble) allow you to upload your art and have it for sale on a variety of products, all through their platform. Then when an item sells, they manufacture the product (print on demand) and handle order fulfillment, giving you a small portion of the proceeds.

I am not a fan of this model for several reasons. For one, there is no branding differentiating the art from other Artists on the site. It's all under the host's branding, which seems generic to me. I also like to ensure a "branded" unpacking experience with each of my orders, with a personalized note and brand card. This is not possible with this type of service. Finally, I'd rather promote my own website and grow my own brand than that of a print-on-demand website's platform.

Gallery Consignment

Pros	Cons
• Monthly check in the mail = consistent income stream.	• Business takes ~50 percent of the retail sale price in *most* cases—not a great profit margin.
• Visibility—another way to get your art in front of new customers (B2C exposure).	• Gallery may not allow you to have the work hanging in their gallery and for sale on your website at the same time.
• There's less heavy lifting (the gallery is selling your work for you).	• Product sits there until it sells, requiring an up-front investment to keep the gallery stocked.

A Note on Galleries

I currently show my work at two galleries and find this to be a great reliable and consistent income stream.

Wholesale

Pros	Cons
• Consistent account = consistent income.	• It can be hard to make a profit off merch when giving a 50 percent wholesale discount.
• Payouts from wholesale accounts can be much larger sums than a sale to a customer (B2B vs. B2C).	• You need to have a backstock of product to fulfill wholesale orders, and it can be hard to predict what wholesalers will order.
• This provides a way for new customers to find your business (B2C exposure).	• Wholesaling products makes less per sale than direct sales.
• You set the rules for minimums/MSRP.	• You have to keep your pricing competitive with similar products for wholesalers to be interested in carrying your product.

What is Wholesale?

Wholesale is when you sell your merchandise to a business/store-front at wholesale pricing. The industry standard for wholesale pricing is 50 percent off retail sales per unit, but you get to set the minimum quantity of units that need to be purchased for the business to receive the wholesale discount. Wholesale is a great way to create another consistent income stream.

I have several accounts that consistently order products throughout the year and have found wholesale to be a lucrative income stream. However, I *never* wholesale my originals, and I occasionally wholesale prints.

For my wholesale accounts, I create a seasonal catalog and order sheets for wholesale that list available merch, product minimums, and cost. For example, to purchase stickers, you must order at least twenty units to receive wholesale pricing at $2.50 per unit, and the store must sell them for an MSRP of $5.00 each.

Licensing

Pros	Cons
• Low overhead cost—the brand invests in the product so you don't have to (B2B).	• Contract negotiations can be confusing and costly, and lawyers are expensive.
• There is potential for a big payout.	• The brand's agenda is to make money. An individual customer purchases your art because they like it, whereas a brand sees it as a profitable investment . . . it's easier to convince someone to buy a print for $50 than to convince a brand to spend $10,000.
• Creating a strong relationship with a successful brand can lead to more deals.	
• Royalty vs. flat fee: either can be successful and profitable based on the payout and terms of your contract.	• There are barriers to entry. If you don't yet have a reputation as an Artist, it can be difficult to begin.
	• If you lack business and negotiation experience, working with brands can be tricky.

Events

Pros	Cons
• You can forge real-life and real-time connections with customers and fans.	• Events can be time intensive and expensive. How far away is the event? Do you have to get a hotel? Do you have someone to help you with setup and breakdown?
• Events can be inspiring and high energy—showing your art at a positive event can generate energy.	
• If the event is a success, your sales are likely to be a success.	• Poor event turnout can make the whole ordeal feel like a waste of time and energy.
• You can draw in new customers to your social media/email newsletter with signups.	• If the event is a flop, or not the right fit for your brand, your sales will be a flop.
	• Event fees can be pricey.

A Note on Events

I've found events are a great way to get my art in front of the public and in front of brands in a lighthearted and casual manner. After all, you never know who you are talking to.

I love events. I love getting the chance to talk with the public and see people's reactions to my art in real time. It's quite amazing. Events are also a fun way to collaborate with a brand in a more casual and laid-back setting. But not all events are created equal. Selecting the right event is important. I've found my success at an event can come down to *who* is throwing the event, *what hours* the event runs, and the *location* you are placed in the event.

Types of Events:

- Festivals: typically multiday with a booth.
- Pop-up shop: set up a merch table for a day/evening.
- Brand collaboration: for example, live painting and a merch table.

In-Person Vending at Events

Whether I am live painting at an event with a merch table, or running a full-on booth at a festival, I always enjoy selling my art in person, as I find the human connection inspiring. There's nothing better than watching a couple pick out their favorite print and decide on the spot where they are going to hang it in their home.

Setting up a pop-up shop/booth and creating a real-life brand aesthetic can be rewarding, and well-attended events can be quite profitable. Typically I promote the event on Instagram ahead of time, so I often have fans in the area come out to say hi, which makes events extra special thanks to the human connection.

Some Artists rely on in-person vending as their main source of income, often going from one event to the next. I prefer to attend only a few events per year, or else I begin to feel burned out on packing my stuff up, setting up, and then breaking down and unpacking. For me, my career has been all about creating a balance, which is why I've enjoyed dabbling in events.

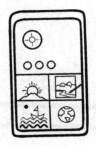

CHAPTER 6

Marketing

Just tell your story. That's all you have to do.

What Is Marketing?

Marketing is the act of promoting and selling your products. To successfully market, you must strategically place your brand in front of an aligned group of consumers and influence them to buy your product. Throughout my career, I have also used marketing to connect with my audience. This type of connection has been vital to the success and visibility of my brand. As we dive into marketing, it's important to start thinking about *making a connection with your audience.*

Types of Marketing

Direct Marketing

Direct marketing influences B2C relationships. When I release a new product, it is marketed in such a way as to inspire people to purchase it.

Example: I send out a newsletter to my email subscribers that describes why the product is important and shows the product displayed in an aesthetic way, with a buy button leading to my website at the bottom. The goal of this type of marketing is to make a sale.

Indirect Marketing

Indirect marketing influences both B2C and B2B relationships, but it does not include a call to action or sale of a product. This is where the connections are built with your audience. Now more than ever, consumers want to make purchases that align with their *values*. Incorporate your business's core values into your marketing so that customers know what you're all about. The bottom line? Put your brand out there in the world on various platforms, and trust that the right people will come to you.

I've found it best to focus on indirect marketing to build my brand, and then when I have something specific to sell, I employ direct marketing.

Examples of ways to market:

1. Facebook business page posts
2. Instagram posts

3. Email newsletter
4. Event outreach
5. Podcast interviews
6. Storefront
7. YouTube videos

From posting on social media to live painting in front of a crowd to van-build YouTube videos to getting interviewed for an article, there are many ways I have connected with my audience.

Connecting with an audience requires constant ingenuity. I have found that marketing in and of itself requires just as much creativity as my art practice. My main marketing tactic throughout the years has been storytelling on Instagram. Since marketing has been the thread sewing the stories of my life together throughout my twenties, I do credit some of the reasoning behind the radical life decisions I have made to the fact that they would tell a good story. And let me tell you, I sure as hell want to *live* a good story.

To be honest with you, I didn't know anything about marketing or branding when I became an Artist. That probably doesn't surprise you by now. But I saw an opportunity: Instagram. I thought acquiring a following could be helpful in my journey to become a Professional Artist. At that time, in 2016, there weren't many Artists on Instagram. After posting a few photos of my art and myself with my art, my following and engagement began to grow. I thought to myself, "If I keep doing this, there is a chance I might actually grow a real following on here." Photo shoots and photo editing became an integral part of my work in the beginning as a Working Artist.

It all began one spring day with my mom's help. She had a nice camera and enjoyed shooting photography as a hobby. After leaving Montana and moving back in with my parents, I had just finished a painting of Mount Rainier, and we spent the morning shooting photos in our yard and then editing my favorites. I made a post on my personal Instagram account of me holding the painting, with a caption that read something like, "Stoked to be back in the PNW." The post got triple the likes that I normally received. I even got some new followers.

We began to re-create this simple formula. Whether it was a photo of me painting or holding a painting, we shot hundreds of photos per concept just to get the perfect one. The perfectionist in me came out with a vengeance. I wanted the art to look bright and bold, and the setting to be spotless. I wanted myself to look flawless. I was frustrated when I couldn't get the right angle. I knew exactly how I wanted the photo to look, but it was often difficult to achieve my vision (hence why we shot hundreds of photos at a time). From there, I would select the best few photos and edit them in Adobe Lightroom. *Huge shout-out to my mom for shooting all those photos of me through the first year that I posted on Instagram. I couldn't have done it without her.*

With storytelling captions, elements of the Pacific Northwest and van life, and high-quality photos, my presence on Instagram grew. Suddenly I was receiving DMs from strangers who wanted to buy my art, and DMs from So You Wanna Bes wondering how I was doing it. Little did they know that my mom was behind the scenes taking all my photos. But it couldn't go on like this forever . . . me living at my mom's house and shooting photos in our backyard. I needed to e x p a n d. I had just bought a van and was ready to hit the road. But who was going to take my photos while I was away?

That's when a college acquaintance, Kory, messaged saying he was heading in my direction on a surf trip, and that he would be stoked to shoot some videos and photos of me and my art. *Was it fate?* I think so. Life has a way of gifting you just what you need when you need it. Kory and I met up on the coast a few weeks later, him in his Subaru and me in my 1987 camper van (named Bentley). Right off the bat, we clicked. So we hopped in my van and went on a month-long trip down the coast. Not only had I found a photographer, but I had found my person. Kory and I are still happily together today. He is my best friend, adventure buddy, business confidant, life partner, and complimentary photographer.

After I consistently posted on Instagram for a few years, guess what . . . my plan worked! Posting high-quality photos grew my audience and my brand. People were buying my art.

Building Your Personal Brand

Marketing and personal branding go hand in hand with selling your products and building your reputation as an Artist. Just as your art has a unique style, your brand has a style. From your logo to your messaging to your product photo aesthetics, this and more builds your personal brand.

Not everyone would agree that you need to be a "brand" to be a Professional Artist. In fact, I had a conversation with someone recently who believes that Artists are not brands. There are many different types of Artists in the world, and I can't speak to all of them. So I'll stick with covering what I know best—my own career.

My business is a **brand** that sells **art**, and my brand name is Gianna Andrews Art. I have built the success of my business off being a successful personal brand, and I believe that in this day and age, the better your branding, the more reputable your art has the potential to become.

Key Elements to Building Your Brand:
- Your unique style as an Artist
- Memorable brand story
- Unique and recognizable logo / Artist signature
- Mission statement and core values used in brand messaging
- Product photo aesthetic
- Unique customer experience (website design, newsletters, social media posts)

Key elements of my brand include the Pacific Northwest, story-telling, outdoor sports like surfing, and van life. I have developed these elements by telling my story on Instagram.

Storytelling Content

My main marketing strategy to connect with my audience has been sharing my story on Instagram. I have strung along my story of being an Artist and an adventurer through the years. It's always amazing to me when I meet people who can recall so much of my story, and it just shows the power of storytelling when building a personal brand.

I never went to business school and never took a marketing course, so I am not sure what they would tell you about marketing budgets or ad dollars. But here are two marketing secrets I've used that they won't teach you in school . . .

Secret #1: You don't necessarily need to spend money on advertising. *I've never spent money on advertising.*

Secret #2: Tell your story. *I've simply just told my story.*

Here is a *Reader's Digest* version of the entire story line I've used in my marketing, from the beginning to where I am today: It all began when I broke my back mountain biking in Montana—that's where I discovered my love for art. Next I moved back to the Pacific

Northwest and finished college. Then I moved to a cabin near Stevens Pass for a ski season, but I ran out of money because all I was doing was skiing and painting, not actually selling my art, so I moved back in with my parents. I slept in a tent in their backyard and spent the summer painting and working at a restaurant.

While still living with my parents, I was given a free trailer and attempted to fix it up, but I ended up getting rid of it because it was too infested with mice. I continued saving up money and bought a 1987 Chevrolet camper van, which I named Bentley. Then I quit my restaurant job and met up with Kory on the coast. We went on a month-long surfing van trip to California (I was brand new to surfing at the time). Again I found myself running out of money, and I was having trouble starting my art business from the van.

I sold Bentley and used the cash to move with Kory into a two-bedroom rental on the Olympic Peninsula. The second bedroom became my art studio. A few months later, we were already missing van life, so we bought a 1995 Ford Aerostar named Rhonda from a friend for $800. It was a downgrade from Bentley, so to spruce things up I taught myself how to spray-paint and covered the van with art over the course of a weekend.

Kory and I started feeling restless for adventure in our rental, so we moved out and drove down the West Coast for the second time, this time in our painted van. We made it to LA, where we sold Rhonda and boarded a one-way flight to Mexico. There we lived with friends in a casita for over a month, and then flew to Baja, rented a car, and camped on the beach. Eventually I got tired of the heat and missed having an art studio, so we flew back to the PNW.

We missed van life, so we found a great deal on a 1978 Dodge camper van, purchased it, gave it a basic build, and named it Blueberry. Not long after, we found a place to live through a family friend—a cabin in the woods that was being reclaimed by nature. So we rolled up our sleeves and got to work, turning the cabin into a magical hobbit-style oasis. It had electricity, a woodburning stove, and no running water. While living there, we adopted our dog, Arrow. We ended up selling Blueberry.

Once the pandemic hit, we had no way to shower, so I bought a house on the Olympic Peninsula, the place we loved and missed. The property has an outbuilding that serves as my art studio. Kory traded in his Subaru for a lifted 2000 Chevy Astro. I purchased a 2021 ProMaster City, which I spent a good portion of 2022 building out with the help of friends. So, yeah, now we each own our own van. That gets you up to speed on where I am today, writing this book. *Whew!* It's been a winding road, but I am so happy I've made it to where I am, and I can't wait to continue sharing what's next.

Why Is Storytelling So Effective?

At the end of the day, we are all human. I think people like to see the Artist behind the art, because it gives them a human-level connection with your work. *Authenticity* might be an overused buzzword, but how can you be *real* in your marketing efforts? This might be the key to your success.

Important note: You get to decide what you keep private about your story and what you make public. There are many things that have happened to me and in my lifetime that have not been a part of my marketing story. Sure, I might be saving them for another book, but that's a side note. ;)

Connecting with Your Audience

Knowing which type of people (your audience) connect with your story and your marketing will help you further craft your content, marketing messaging, and overall brand to fit this mold. It can be helpful to focus on a single audience to ensure your branding/marketing is cohesive. For me, not only has knowing my audience helped me develop my content to appeal to them, but it has also guided the subject matter of my artwork.

When I began developing my style, I had two clear themes. One was the developed brand you see today: whimsical, nature-inspired art. The other was a more PG-13 version . . . provocative lips, grillz, and skulls (I call that side G-Spice) . . . I realized that in order to be really successful I had to narrow in on an audience, because I quickly learned that there wasn't a crossover between the young outdoor-lover athlete and the rap-music-loving young person. My sapling of a brand was divided, with the potential to appeal to two very different audiences and different types of people. I had a decision to make.

Who did I want to be publicly? Which part of my personality and style did I want to promote and be visible to thousands of people? I had a feeling that my art was going to be big no matter what, and I knew I was going to be a Professional Artist one day soon, but I also knew I couldn't move forward with both of these puzzle pieces that didn't quite fit together.

I don't remember when I made the shift or if it just occurred naturally, but I suppose my brand became more cohesive with a tad more life experience and some van life adventures. It felt like a natural transition to focus on nature art. Do I miss G-Spice at times? Sure. But she's always with me, and she still gets to inspire my art. Plus, I believe it's healthy to keep a sliver of yourself that isn't plastered all over the internet. For me, that's G-Spice.

You see? The more specific you can be, especially in the beginning, before you've established yourself as a reputable Artist, the easier it will be to grow your following and, in turn, sell your art. **Cohesion is key.**

Customer Journey

For a customer to purchase a product, you must have somewhere the sale can take place. Let's say you make a creative Instagram post, where you may or may not use a direct marketing tactic, encouraging people to check out your website or product page.

You get five hundred likes, and out of those five hundred people who liked it, fifty of them click the link to go on your website. Out of those fifty people, twenty-five of them add something to their cart. Out of those twenty-five people, fourteen complete the sale by making a purchase. This is your customer journey. I have more than thirty thousand followers on Instagram. Of them, several thousand have made purchases to date.

Haters

I'm here to burst your bubble: not everyone is going to love your art. Not everyone is going to love you. *Especially* once you start putting yourself out there with cohesive brand messaging. The more attention you receive from people who love your brand, the more likely you will have some people who also dislike your brand. And that's **okay**. My advice in dealing with my fair share of haters? Rise above. It sounds cliché, but it's true. Don't ever let someone else's negativity take your power away. It's harder than it sounds, because one bad comment can sting through hundreds of nice comments. But if you're here to please everyone, kindly abort mission now. 'Cause once you have haters, that's when you know you've *made it*.

Fans

If you continually build your art portfolio, your personal brand, and your audience, I promise that people are going to connect with your art. I promise that people are going to love you, the Artist behind the art. Some of these people will become fans who support you, and some will become superfans who absolutely love you.

Fan

A fan is one of your supporters who shows up to your offerings, owns some of your product, and keeps up to date with your brand. Fans are typically repeat customers and probably tell their friends about your work. Your fans are important to your business, so you need to treat then well and incentivize them to remain supporters with extra perks such as thank-you notes.

Superfan

A superfan belongs to a small fan subgroup that engages with virtually everything and anything you do. They purchase every new product you release. They own your high-value items. They drive hours to show up at your events. They know your whole story and love your brand. They tell all their friends about you.

It's important to identify who your superfans are and keep them happy. Every holiday I write my superfans an email with a super-special discount code that only they receive. Last New Year's, I sent them individual handwritten letters. Every time someone purchases an original, I include a handwritten card and sticker pack. It's important to make sure they know that they matter.

Your fans and your superfans are the backbone supporters of your business. Having a core audience builds a resilient brand.

Collectors

Collectors are a superfan subgroup who collect your original pieces. I have one superfan who has purchased more than fifteen of my original paintings. Wow! I think of collectors as guardian angels. They consistently support you and your work, and that means the world to me. It is beyond an honor to have collectors.

Ways to Keep Fans Engaged:

- Handwritten thank-you notes with every order
- Fan-only discount codes
- Holiday thank-you cards
- Extra swag with orders
- Appreciation

Creating Change with Social Media

The point of being an Artist is not to amass a huge social media following. The goal of creating art is to connect with people individually and use your art as a catalyst for instigating *change*. Social media can be a great tool to share your core values and mission statement to instigate change. But it is not the end all, be all.

I was able to make the world a little bit better by sharing my messaging on Instagram. And once that impact became uninspiring to me, I began pursuing new avenues to instigate change.

If you find a social media platform that allows you to connect with others and instigate change, as I did with Instagram a few years back, that is amazing. You don't need one hundred thousand followers to do this. Heck, you don't need ten thousand followers. You just need a core group of people who are inspired by your purpose. It's possible to have both—a huge internet presence and a soul-led art practice. But is everyone doing that on the internet? Nope, definitely not.

How to Grow a Social Media Presence

Reminder: Having a strong internet presence does not mean you are a *good* Artist. It means you are good at marketing and branding. Not having a social media presence does not mean you are a *bad* Artist. It means you are probably not very good at marketing and branding . . . yet! So let's cover how to market yourself on the internet.

Growing a social media following is all about finding the platform that works best for you. And then doubling down on being YOU. Just as you need to focus on developing your own unique style as an Artist, you need to hone in on developing your own unique style as a marketer. How can you be unique to you, your style, your soul? As we covered before, tell your story, because no one else has your unique story. Tag team your story with your unique art style and you are likely to gain traction on the internet.

It's not easy to create unique, authentic, and consistent content. But to grow a social media presence, you must. There are a lot of different social media platforms out there, including YouTube,

TikTok, and Facebook. The key is to choose the one that works best for you and focus your marketing efforts there.

The Social Media Growth Formula—QUAC

Quality: Post quality work and quality content. Pixilated, blurry, or busy photos/video do not transfer well to a small screen.

Unique: Be different! Be you! Share something only you can share.

Authentic: Ensure your content is true to your core values and mission statement. This is true authenticity that people crave.

Consistent: People are going to follow you so they can see your future posts, so it's important to continue to consistently engage with your audience.

If you stick with this QUAC formula, there is great potential to grow an audience and boost your reputation as an Artist. Decide on the content that you can consistently create and share it with those on your chosen social media platform.

Pro Tip 1: It's important to maintain some privacy and boundaries around your life, and everyone's boundaries on what they are willing to share will be different.

Pro Tip 2: Try to avoid following along on a trend that other people are already doing on a given social media platform. Be a TRENDSETTER! This is what is going to set you apart.

My Relationship with Instagram

At the beginning, I made paintings and posted them on Instagram. It was simple but effective, and from there the entire business expanded. I began sharing my art and story on Instagram in 2016, over six years ago. It took me about a year to evolve my brand cohesion, as I was posting both mountains and G-Spice-inspired art. Once I let go of G-Spice and dialed in my marketing messaging, my audience grew quickly from less than one thousand followers to more than twenty thousand. I had perfected my posting formula, and it worked effectively for several years.

I don't think my career would be where it is today without working really hard to market myself on Instagram for all those years. Instagram allowed me to reach people nationally and internationally that otherwise wouldn't have seen my work. It allowed me to become a Professional Artist who supports my livelihood off my creativity. I am proud of the work I published on the app and thankful for the connections I've made there.

My following began to plateau toward the end of 2021, reaching thirty thousand. There are a lot of reasons my growth plateaued on the app, from the fact that I hit a mountain-art-trend bubble that may have popped due to oversaturation, to changes in the algorithm, to the fact that I post much less than I used to.

Since I now have established income streams, I rely less on Instagram to get my personal brand message out there. In general, I am less concerned about growing an internet following than I used to be, so I put in less effort. My photo shoots are not anywhere near as extensive as they were back in the day. Now I focus on sharing when I have something important to share, versus posting every day.

My relationship with Instagram has changed significantly over the past six years. Heck, I've changed significantly over the past six years. Posting on Instagram used to make me *feel like I was making a difference in people's lives*, like I was inspiring other people to be better versions of themselves. To become Artists, to follow their soul calling, to take care of the planet . . . all pieces of my core values.

Then about a year and a half ago, I began to get uninspired by my posting routine of shooting hundreds of photos. I was sick of the whole app in general. I began feeling like *people didn't care about my art like they used to*. And if people didn't care, then what difference did it make if I post or not? On top of that, I felt as though I was missing out on enjoying my life, because I was always trying to capture the moment by getting the right photo. I was exhausted from the pressure I felt to "sell myself." I was tired of nit-picking my body to look good on a screen. I was comparing myself to Artists who were getting more likes than me.

During my Instagram journey, I transitioned from a passionate, naive Working Artist, living in my parents' house, into a full-blown Professional Artist. From far-off dreams came reality—a reality in which I rely upon my art to feed myself, pay my mortgage, and support the lifestyle I desire. Sometimes it hits me like a brick that my creativity is responsible for paying all my bills. Putting all that pressure on each post on Instagram started to wear me down. It felt like if I wasn't doing well on the 'gram, then it meant my business was failing. I felt confined to the four walls of the app.

So I've taken time to practice what I preach and spend more time living in the moment. I've created new boundaries with myself and Instagram. I now spend less time on my phone. I post much less. I scroll less. And guess what? My career is still thriving, and my business is still growing.

To this day, I still use Instagram, and I still post when I have something to share. But in a way I feel like I've outgrown it. Like the whole concept of curating my life for the app no longer matters *as much* to me as it once did (we'd be lying if we said it didn't matter a little, right?).

I am an Artist, after all, not an Instagram robot. **What truly matters to me is that I create change and help the world become a better place.** Which is why I decided to write this book and share it with you.

Believe

It's not an easy road to follow your soul calling.

It's going to feel like you are free-falling.

Can you trust it?

Or will you keep stalling?

You did it! You've already made leaps and bounds in your journey to becoming an Artist by reading this book. You know what steps you need to take. Now it's time to start listening to your *soul calling* and then putting in the *work* to make that dream a reality. From developing your own unique style to implementing a creative practice to building out your business, making products, and marketing your art, it goes without saying that there's a lot of work to be done. But I did it, and that means you can do it too!

I sincerely hope both the tools and personal anecdotes in this book have inspired you to strive to become the best version of an Artist that you can be. Remember, *it's not an easy road, baby*, once you become an Artist. But it's well worth the rewards, because as an Artist, you get to be a change maker in this world. You get to create your own universal laws and follow your own core values . . . Does it get any more rewarding than that? You were put here for a reason, and that reason might just be art!

The question becomes, *Will you trudge down this slightly bush-whacked path I laid out for you, or will you continue down the road of a rock and a hard place?* Only you can decide to live out your soul calling.

I believe in you. The question becomes, *Do you believe in yourself?*

About the Author

Hey, **I'm Gianna!** Born and raised on a tiny island in the Pacific Northwest, my art is influenced by a lifetime of exploring nature surrounding me—the forest, mountains, and ocean.

Though the outdoors have been an important aspect of my life since I can remember, it wasn't until later that art entered my life. I followed my passion of outdoor sports to attend college in Bozeman, Montana, where on a whim I enrolled in an art class. My fascination with art grew—enough to stay in the art studio all night, struggling to master one little piece of a painting.

However, my love story with art did not fully develop until I had a terrible mountain biking wreck, resulting in a broken back, broken teeth, and abrasions covering my body. Suddenly I found myself stripped of the freedom that I was accustomed to experiencing in my outdoor adventures. Confined to a hard plastic back brace for months, I spent my recovery at the easel, finding solace and freedom in painting my favorite outdoor scenery instead of exploring it.

Now, years later, I haven't stopped painting. Art has blossomed into not only my greatest passion but also a successful career. By sharing my art and story with the world, I hope to inspire others to become the best version of themselves and realize their dreams, even during the darkest of times, when these things seem most out of reach.

For More Art & Story

giannaandrews.com

▶ Gianna Andrews

📷 @giannaandrews

f Gianna Andrews Art

♪ @gianna.andrews